"George Merlis knows everything about blasting through the background sound and making your point. He is not just a great coach for acing a media interview. His rules work for all of life. You can use them on TV, at meetings, on job interviews, on dates, or ordering a pizza by phone! He's talking about being the most effective you."
— DIANE SAWYER, ABC NEWS

"The well-prepared interviewer can control the focus and content of an interview with an ill-prepared interviewee. On the other hand, the well-prepared interviewee can always get his message across, no matter how skilled the interviewer. George Merlis's fine book details how to meet the media and prevail."
— DAVID HARTMAN, ORIGINAL HOST,
GOOD MORNING AMERICA

"Being media savvy is an essential survival skill in the 21st century. I am constantly amazed at the smart, successful people who stumble and stammer when a camera is pointed in their face. George Merlis's book will help media neophytes become media pros".
— LEONARD MALTIN, FILM JOURNALIST,
CRITIC AND HISTORIAN

"Written concisely, expertly, entertainingly, and — above all — helpfully, George Merlis's book reveals the secrets of what goes into a good interview and builds up the reader's confidence to plunge into the media fray. The result? Even I'm ready for my close-up, Mr. DeMille."
— STEPHEN M. SILVERMAN, EDITOR
PEOPLE MAGAZINE'S people.com DAILY

MERLIS ON MEDIA MASTERY

HOW TO MASTER THE MEDIA v2.0

MAKING YOUR MESSAGE COUNT
ON THE AIR, IN PRINT, AND ONLINE

BY GEORGE MERLIS

JAAND BOOKS, LOS ANGELES, CA
WWW.MASTERTHEMEDIA.COM

LIBRARY OF CONGRESS Cataloging-in-Publication Data

Merlis, George, 1940-
    Merlis on Media Mastery
    How to Master the Media v2.0

    p.   cm.
    includes index.
    ISBN 978-0-9906749-0-0
    1. media training 2. interviews 3. interviewing on
    television 4. interviewing in journalism
    5. media interviews 6. crisis communications
    7. Title.

CONTENTS

CHAPTER 1

MEET AND MASTER THE MEDIA

> **"In the future everyone will be famous for fifteen minutes."**
>
> *Andy Warhol, The Andy Warhol Diaries, July, 1978*

Today, the media's insatiable appetite for material is growing in a geometric progression, and the media universe - the constellations of outlets disseminating news and information - is expanding so fast it's impossible to track. Looking back, Warhol's bold 1978 prediction is today's naïve understatement. Are *you* prepared for *your* fifteen minutes? What about the altogether likely possibility that your fifteen minutes may stretch into fifteen hours, fifteen days, or even fifteen weeks of media attention? It could happen.

> **"In a world where everyone with a cellphone camera is paparazzi, everyone with access to Twitter... is a reporter and everyone who can upload video on YouTube is a filmmaker, everyone else is a public figure — and fair game."**
> *— Thomas L. Friedman, The New York Times, May 20 , 2014*

1

As Tom Friedman notes, today nearly everyone can be a self-appointed journalist. Newsmakers learn this fact after making unguarded comments in semi-private places, and then finding those statements in the mainstream media via Twitter, Facebook, blogs and YourTube.

In 2008, then-Senator and Presidential candidate Barack Obama learned that lesson the hard way when a blogger at a West Coast fundraiser recorded him saying of discouraged blue collar voters: "It's not surprising, then, they get bitter, they cling to guns or religion or antipathy to people who aren't like them or anti-immigrant sentiment or anti-trade sentiment as a way to explain their frustrations." (The blogger, who did not identify herself, recorded that moment only on audio, but you can hear it to this day on YouTube.) Four years later, at another fundraiser, this one in Florida, GOP Presidential candidate Mitt Romney repeated Mr. Obama's indiscretion, telling a group of wealthy supporters that 47 percent of the people would not vote for him because they were dependent on the government. He added, "My job is not to worry about those people. I'll never convince them they should take personal responsibility for their lives." He was clandestinely recorded on cell phone video The Romney recording was made by the bartender hired for the fund-raiser, who posted it on YouTube, where it resided in obscurity until it was discovered by a journalist (interestingly enough, former President Jimmy Carter's grandson) who wrote about it for Mother Jones. Thereafter it went viral, global and became a major campaign issue.

The lesson here is that anyone can be a media representative or source. You don't have to be caught in an unguarded moment to find yourself in an unflattering media spotlight. In fact, these unguarded moments are less common than traditional media encounters. The basic currency of those media encounters is the interview. Master the interview and you master the media.

These days, the media cast wide nets and if one of those nets ensnares you, you have two basic choices: to willingly comply with the reporter's agenda - which may or may not mesh with your own - or to master the situation by taking control and working the encounter to your advantage. The difference between compliance and mastery is the set of skills and the body of knowledge presented in this book.

In these pages I've used everything I've learned in my forty year long broadcast and print career to help you master your media encounters. That career has encompassed a lot of interviews. I have conducted or overseen more than 10,000 print and broadcast interviews in my years as a reporter, editor, and TV producer. They have run the gamut from friendly chats on "Good Morning America" to tough, adversarial confrontations on investigative TV news magazines. I've interviewed a vast number of individuals myself and I've researched, produced, and written major stories - including exposés - for newspapers, magazines, and television networks. Whatever the interview, I always wanted my interview subject to do a good job, to express herself well. Why? Well, it made my job a lot easier if I could use her words instead of mine, if I could quote her rather than paraphrase her. Even with the best of intentions, every reporter knows that when he paraphrases, he is also filtering — filtering his interview subject's ideas through his knowledge and perceptions.

As a reporter and a producer, I would listen to every answer and mentally put it into one of three pigeon holes:

Using the knowledge gained in my media career, I have created a curriculum designed to give you the tools to turn all your interview responses into *Gotta Use That* answers.

I have media trained a large and diverse number of spokespersons for more than thirty years. I am the go-to trainer for NASA's Science Mission Directorate as well as for every major recording label in the country, so my clients range - quite literally - from rock stars to rocket scientists. I distilled what I taught them in a book, **How to Master the Media** and now I've updated and enhanced the material in that book for this volume, **Merlis on Media Mastery; How to Master the Media v2.0.**

I mentioned rock stars and rocket scientists. Well, whether you're one or the other - or you make your living in another sector of the economy - the easily learned communications skills in this updated book will help you reach the public through the media.

The techniques I teach in media training workshops are based on my observations and on practices honed during a full career as reporter, writer, editor, television news producer, and media training consultant. If you are ever interviewed by the media - if you face even a remote prospect of being interviewed - this book will supply you with a storehouse of vital information. A cautionary note: these media mastery skills require practice and repetition because some of them - like beginning your answer with your conclusion instead of building to your conclusion - are counterintuitive for most of us. The biggest mistake you can make is to treat an interview like a conversation. It is not. No matter how skillful the reporter is in appearing casual and off-the-cuff, he is *working* when he's talking to you. You must look at an interview as work, too. The reporter has a job to do: to ferret out information for his story. You also have a job: to be sure that the information he gets from you is the information you *want* him to get, and only that information. I tell my entertainment industry clients to think of an interview not as a conversation, but as a *performance*. "You don't just get up and sing," I tell them. "You know your material, you know the venue, you know your audience. It's the same thing with an interview. Your agenda is your material. Your venue is the reporter's media outlet. And his readers, viewers or listeners are your audience."

There are basic skills — such as speaking in soundbites, illustrating your key points with compelling language, and keeping your answers short, simple, and comprehensible — that you need whether you are preparing for an appearance on a national investigative broadcast magazine like "60 Minutes," you have been booked for a brief product-plugging appearance on a local radio show, or you are facing an in-depth interview by a well-prepared reporter for a national newspaper like the *Washington Post* or *The New York Times*. Anyone who might one day be called upon by the media to defend a point of view, explain a policy, or to promote a project or product needs to learn how to:

¶ Speak to the media the way the media speak to us.
¶ Deliver answers that help both you and the reporter.
¶ Parry a journalist's catalog of dirty tricks.

All this and more are covered in this book. The skills you will learn here include:

¶ Creating your interview agenda.
¶ Working that agenda into the interview.
¶ Protecting yourself in a hostile interview.
¶ Reaching beyond the reporter to the public.

Whether your questions will come from a top national reporter like David Sanger of the New York Times or from a TV star like CNN's Anderson Cooper or from a friendly neighbor who is writing for the local weekly newspaper, an interview is your best opportunity to reach a wide audience with a message. This book teaches you to formulate your messages and to work them gracefully and effectively into any interview. Preparation is the key; it helps you do more than merely survive a media encounter, it enables you to triumph. The set of skills presented in this book can help anyone master the media.

I have designed the book to be a simple step-by-step how-to guide. Whenever possible I've illustrated my points with anecdotes or case histories that serve as object lessons. Periodically I'm going to ask you to do a little homework, such as filling out some worksheets in preparation for an interview. These exercises are critical because they will teach you how to get ready for the real thing. After correctly preparing for your interview, you will feel confident about facing a reporter, whether that questioner is a fawning fan or an aggressive inquisitor. I recommend preparing for all interviews by writing your agenda on a computer, where it can easily be saved and recalled and tweaked for subsequent interviews. And while you're at your computer, you can do the essential research for your agenda, using search engines like Google and the web sites of relevant publications. Today, thanks to these online tools, finding the facts, figures, references, and statistics for use in your agenda is much easier than it was in the old days when we had to thumb through an almanac, an encyclopedia, or other reference book.

A word about how I've organized this book: we'll begin by exploring the basic media mastery skills you'll need whether you're interviewed by a reporter for a newspaper, a magazine, a blog, a company newsletter, or a local or national television news program. These are fundamental communication skills like speaking in complete sentences, keeping your answers concise, and being quoteworthy. You will need to master these skills in order to be a successful interview subject. Then we'll move on to television's unique and specific demands and you will learn the little tricks of the trade that make you a "good guest" or an interesting interview. You'll learn to speak with animation, how to illustrate your points with gestures, and how to engage your interviewer. These television skills are largely matters of style and cosmetics that in no way substitute for substance. They are designed to enhance the essence of what you are saying. Good television style - making yourself an interesting TV speaker - is no different from good writing style. Good style makes your message more palatable and comprehensible whether you are on the page or on the airwaves. As a television viewer you already know this. When you see a bad interview subject, your attention wanders and you absorb little. Watch a good interview subject and your attention remains focused and you take away her principal message points. You will most likely recognize her the next time she is on television and you'll look forward to hearing what she has to say. The good television interview subject informs in an entertaining, engrossing way.

Increasingly, television spokespersons are asked to demonstrate rather than merely talk. More television programs want show-and-tell these days because viewers respond better and remember more if a guest or interview subject can demonstrate as well as talk. So, if you're talking about a new electronic device, you'd better be prepared to demonstrate it. If you're discussing a medical breakthrough, television prefers that you illustrate it by bringing images and narrating over those images. The tricks of this aspect of the spokesperson's trade, which you'll discover in detail later in the book, include knowing how to show objects to a camera, knowing how to move on camera, and knowing how to talk about your subject while demonstrating or illustrating it.

This book also includes specific information on radio interviews, news conferences, and interviews conducted over the phone, via email, and Skype. In the case of radio, you rely only on your voice for communication. You'll learn how to energize your voice, how to make your points concisely, and how to insure the audience knows who is speaking. You'll learn that in a news conference, facing fifteen reporters really is not fifteen times more challenging than facing a single reporter, and you'll learn how to dominate one of these group sessions. You'll see how the telephone — an old technology — and Skype — a very new technology — offer both risks and opportunities. I'll tell you how to avoid the first and take advantage of the second. You'll see how to capitalize on the fact your interviewer cannot see what you're doing so that a phone interview becomes, in effect, an open-book test where you can have lots of helpful material right in front of you. And, surprisingly, you'll learn that although the interviewer *can* see you in a Skype interview, it, too, is an open book test.

I suggest you read the entire book and complete all the exercises well before your first interview. There is a lot of material to absorb here and cramming just before your media "exam" won't work any better than those allnighters you inflicted on yourself before midterms and finals in college. Moreover, you need sufficient time to process your agenda for each specific interview and you don't want that process compromised by speedreading. Let's start with the basics:

WHAT IS NEWS?

You probably think you know what news is. But it's likely you are thinking of the dictionary definition of news. There is also a practical definition of news — one that is more important for our purposes.

THE DICTIONARY DEFINITION
News: A report of a recent event;
intelligence; information.

THE PRACTICAL DEFINITION
News: A report that captures and holds
the attention of an audience.

Spurred by today's cutthroat competition for readers, viewers, and listeners, many media outlets put a premium on the second definition. And there is no better way to capture and hold attention than by playing on emotions. Back in 1914, the columnist known as the Sage of Baltimore, H.L. Mencken, wrote: "Any reflective newspaperman knows that it is hard for plain people to *think* about a thing, but easy for them to *feel*." The rules of the game haven't changed so today we increasingly see many of our reporters, producers, and editors guided by five "f" words, all of them printable in a family newspaper.

THE MEDIA'S FIVE "F" WORDS

Fear
Fury
Fame
Fun
Fascination

Let's examine each of those words:

¶ **Fear.** The media thrive on scare stories. Threatening hurricanes, earthquakes, tornadoes, volcanic eruptions, possible terrorist attacks, and viral pandemics always command attention. During the summer of 2006 the local Los Angeles broadcast media carried frequent alarmist reports about West Nile virus. To hear them you would have thought there was an epidemic. Quite the contrary was true: local health officials had done a very good job of eradicating virus-carrying mosquitoes. But the steady drum beat of broadcast scare stories attracted and held viewers.

Skillful spokespersons use scary language to win converts to their point of view. Take the phrase "death tax," which the levy's opponents use instead of "estate" or "inheritance" tax. The word "death" is frightening. And, since everyone eventually dies, the implication of the phrase "death tax" is that everyone's heirs are subject to it. In point of fact, while about two million Americans die each year, the estates of fewer than 10,000 of them are subject to that tax. By calling it an estate or inheritance tax, opponents would have far less traction in the marketplace of ideas because the words "estate" and "inheritance" are not frightening and, in fact, have an elitist connotation.

¶ **Fury.** The media are highly biased, but the slant isn't universally a political bias as some would have you believe. In fact, President George W. Bush's first press secretary, Ari Fleicher, got it right in the *Washington Post* on January 10, 2005 when he was quoted saying, "My conclusion is the press is biased — biased in favor of conflict. Conflict comes first...." For the media, especially broadcast outlets, a fear-driven conflict is the best kind of story because producers usually can count on at least one side getting highly emotional. Emotion equals drama and drama captures and holds an audience's attention. Thus the emotionally charged pros and cons of that nuclear power plant a utility wants to build a mile away from an elementary school is a great story because it's filled with fear and fury. This bias in favor of controversy sometimes leads the media to indulge in false equivalencies — granting equal weight to legitimate and specious arguments. We often see this in medical stories when outliers with scientifically unsound positions are granted unwarranted expo sure in the interest of "balance." In fact the exposure is granted in the interest of drama.

¶ **Fame.** The media love stories about the famous or those who they can make famous. If cops stop Mrs. Brown from down the street for driving with an unsecured infant on her lap there is no news story. If they bust Britney Spears for the same offense, it's a major story. If an ordinary 19-year-old gets stopped by the police for DUI and drag racing, it's no story. If the teen-ager is Justin Beiber, it becomes a sensation. Similarly, if a cashier at your local big box retailer decides to kidnap and do bodily harm to her romantic rival, it's not much of a story. But if a woman astronaut embarks on such a jealousy-fueled enterprise, it becomes a big story because the media can make her famous due to her career choice.

¶ **Fun.** In our current era of Jon Stewart and his colleagues and imitators, even the dullest local news anchor tries to be funny. If it's funny, it sells. So the story of the jealous woman astronaut got even more attention when it was reported she wore diapers driving from Houston to Orlando to confront her romantic rival in order to skip those time-consuming pit stops. That's funny, right? Never mind the facts: there was hard evidence she made several pit stops on her drive (after all, no car can make it from Houston to Orlando without refueling) and the diapers found in her car were toddler size, unlikely to fit even the smallest astronaut. A word of caution about fun: Comedy is a dangerous business, as we'll see later in this book. Generally it should be left to trained and skilled professionals — comedians.

¶ **Fascination.** Any "Gee, I never knew that" moment, piece of information or gadget appeals to the media. For the vast majority of readers of this book who are not famous, the other "f" words are important, but it is likely none is more important than fascination. If you're not famous and you're dealing with something that has neither a fear factor nor any controversial elements, it's incumbent on you to make it fascinating.

HOW THE MEDIA USE INTERVIEWS

Let's understand just how important an interview is in the construction of a news story. Interviews, whether used as a source for verbatim quotes or just for editorial background and research guidance, are the basis for most of the news stories we read and see. The print media initially perfected the practice of using the interview as the key building block of a story and the technique was adapted by the broadcast media to meet their unique needs.

THE PRINT MEDIA

Print journalists create stories by interviewing a source or a number of sources and then paraphrasing or directly quoting what the sources said. The journalist/writers then combine these quotes and/or paraphrases with other material, including first-hand observations by the reporter or colleagues, press releases, earlier articles, and research from books, other journals, and the Internet. Using all these elements, they craft a narrative story.

Sometimes the story is from a single point of view as in: "The administration says it is taking steps to ensure that NASA has sufficient research funds to examine climate change thoroughly." At other times, the story comes from multiple points of view, as in: "The administration says it is taking steps to insure that NASA has sufficient research funds to examine climate change thoroughly, however congressional sources say that a substantial number of House members and a few Senators don't believe there is any climate change and will oppose authorizations to study the matter." Either way, the finished story will use quotes and paraphrases from various spokespeople to flesh out the account.

Another type of article, the Q&A, is just that: questions asked by a reporter and the interview subject's answers in direct quotes. It is the print media's equivalent of a live broadcast interview. The only editing that occurs in one of these articles is the condensation of some answers and the elimination of questions and answers that, in the reporter's opinion, do not further the flow.

THE BROADCAST MEDIA

Television stories are created by editing together three basic elements: on-camera interviews, on-camera transitions by the reporter, and footage that illustrates elements of the story, which is called B-roll. The B-roll is narrated either by the reporter or by soundbites pulled from the interviews. The narration is called a voiceover; its origin being the phrase "voice over film." Much of the correspondent on-camera and voiceover material will be created by paraphrasing spokespersons' quotations garnered in interviews. The rest will come from the same sorts of research sources the print reporter used. Radio stories are similarly structured, except that they have no B-roll, but instead include bits of so-called "actuality audio," that is non-speaking sound recorded on the scene of the news story. Actuality audio might include the sound of trees being cut down for a story on shrinking rain forests or the sound of cars' motors and horns for a story on traffic congestion.

The following is an example of how television might report the hypothetical NASA story cited above. Notice how the interviews are a key ingredient in the edited news story.

Correspondent on camera in front of the White House: "The administration, saying it is concerned about climate change and global warming, is seeking a supplemental appropriation from Congress for two additional NASA climate-observation missions. If granted, the appropriation will fund more intensive research into the phenomenon, its causes, and its progress."

Animation of an orbiting satellite, the correspondent voiceover: "The White House feels that two more satellite missions like this are needed to compliment the observations of earlier NASA satellites examining global climate change."

White House science advisor, on camera, identified by a "lower-third," a caption giving his name and title: "The President feels that ongoing global climate change will have vast repercussions throughout society and the economy. There are public safety, agricultural, and commercial concerns that we must address. Unless we have adequate information we won't be able to take the needed steps to reduce the warming trend or to accommodate unavoidable consequences of climate change. Without these two new missions we are like surgeons operating in the dark."

B-roll of the Capitol with correspondent voiceover narration: "However, on Capitol Hill, the announcement was greeted with skepticism in some important quarters."

Rep. Rupkins, on-camera soundbite. Lower-third identifies him as chairman of the Ways and Means Committee: "The science is still out on this one, but I can tell you that in my district we have not seen any evidence whatsoever of climate change. This so-called global warming story is the biggest fiction story ever sold to the American people. It ought to be at the top of the New York Times fiction bestseller list. I'm not going to allow this administration boondoggle to get to the floor because those two missions would be a waste of taxpayer dollars."

Closing summation from correspondent in front of the White House: "So the battle is joined. The administration claims that failure to fund these two missions will cost the United States dearly in the future, while Rep. Rupkins, representing a powerful group of lawmakers who are climate change skeptics and even deniers, says he needs proof of global climate change before he will allow a vote on funding the missions. For now, the purse strings are tied and the administration is searching for a strategy to loosen them."

You can see how the two interviews supplied the spine for the story and how the controversy played a large part in making the report more dramatic. Both spokespersons got in lines that made their soundbites memorable. The science advisor used the simile of the surgeons operating in the dark and the congressman used the metaphor of global warming being the biggest fiction story ever sold to the American public. These were "grabbers" and I'll deal with them in depth later on.

LIVE BROADCAST INTERVIEWS

Whether they are broadcast on radio or television, live interviews are segments in which a host interviews a subject for a specific length of time (usually with breaks only for commercials) and, in some cases, invites viewer or listener call-in questions. The interview may be long or short. For example, my *alma mater*, "Good Morning America," and the other morning programs used to schedule interviews to run between five and eight minutes. Today, those morning show interviews rarely run five minutes at their longest. A generation of viewers reared watching MTV and 30-second commercials has learned to absorb information in very brief bursts, and the interview shows are accommodating that shortened attention span. Many viewers won't tolerate longer interviews; they demand that subject and venue change quickly and often. Perhaps we are a nation suffering from mass attention deficit disorder. Or perhaps we've all learned how to quickly grasp and process a rapid-fire flow of information. Whether that's a curse or a blessing I'll leave to social scientists and psychologists. For our purposes it's sufficient to know that the short form live interview is a fact of broadcast life today and spokespersons must learn to communicate concisely.

Of course, there remain broadcasts like "Charlie Rose" on PBS and "Fresh Air" on NPR which will often give over a whole hour or a substantial portion of an entire hour to a single guest or a small group of guests. If you are lucky enough to rate an invitation to sit at Charlie Rose's round table or to talk with Fresh Air host Terry Gross, you are virtually guaranteed that most, if not all, of what you say in the interview will make it to air.

Whatever the length, a live or live-to-tape TV or radio interview gives you the most control, since it goes out to the audience unedited or only lightly edited. The opportunity is there, but so is the challenge. There is no second chance in a live interview, no calling up after the fact and saying, "There's something else you should know...." So it's incumbent on you to get it right the first time, and the skills you learn in these pages will help you to do that.

NEW MEDIA INTERVIEWS

New media, Internet-borne information, take a number of forms. There are email interviews — in effect an emailed exchange of questions and answers with little opportunity for a reporter to catch you off guard if you are careful. There are chatrooms and there are Skype interviews. I'll deal with these later on, but the basic rules for mastery in these, as in older media formats, are the same.

I want this book to be your Bible for media encounters. To that end, let's begin with what I like to call the commandments of interviews. There are five of them; I did not have the temerity to go for ten:

THE FIVE COMMANDMENTS OF INTERVIEWS

I. Thou shalt be prepared.
II. Thou shalt know thy listener.
III. Thou shalt be quoteworthy.
IV. Thou shalt practice, practice, practice.
V. Thou Shalt Not Lie, Evade, nor Cop an Attitude.

These five commandments should be your mantra when you prepare for any media appearance. I'll discuss them in detail in the next two chapters. Keeping the commandments foremost in your mind and putting them into practice will go a long way toward assuring successful media appearances.

No doubt you have read the assertion that most people fear public speaking appearances more than they fear death. How much more public can an appearance be than a news media interview? And the fact of the matter is we may have to make numerous public appearances, but we only die once. So whether the fear of an interview or speech is greater than, on a par with, or even less than the fear of dying, it certainly is a more frequently encountered dread. It is quite likely that the cause of both fears is the feeling that in these situations we exercise little or no control. That's where this book comes in — at least in public appearance situations. It will help you overcome the fear of interviews and other public speaking events by giving you the tools to take control. When you get through these pages, you'll lose your fear and you'll view media appearances as opportunities, not as threats. The skill set you will learn here will level the media playing field, or even tilt it in your favor.

Over the years I've observed that the most successful interview subjects are men and women who, regardless of what they're speaking about, approach their media encounters with a sense of purpose, a positive — even eager — attitude, and an enthusiasm for their subject. For some outgoing and passionately committed people this attitude comes naturally. For others, this is learned behavior. While I may appear to be describing the ideal television guest, you should bear in mind that the reporter interviewing you for the local newspaper is — like the television viewer — an audience, too. If you can engage a hundred thousand or a million people in a television appearance, the same skills and attitude will enable you to engage that reporter, your audience of one. Successful interview subjects consciously or unconsciously heed a certain interview discipline. To embrace that discipline, you'll need to learn and obey the five commandments of interviews.

Let's begin our journey to media mastery with the most essential fundamental: preparation. In Chapter 2, you'll learn how to prepare for any interview as I explain the Boy Scout commandments. This chapter will help you create an agenda for an interview. Your agenda is key; without one you are at the mercy of the reporter and he may or may not help you out. With an agenda you can master the media.

THE BOY SCOUT COMMANDMENTS

I call the first two commandments of interviews the Boy Scout Commandments because they take their inspiration from scouting's famous motto, "Be Prepared."

If the term *commandments* seems strong, that's intentional. You don't want to leave your interview performance to chance, so you must play by a strict set of rules. The most effective spokespersons are those who are dedicated to getting out their message in a manner that is simultaneously engaging, comprehensive, and comprehensible. Becoming that  messenger requires dedication as well as strict adherence to the commandments.

To illustrate the importance of preparation, let me tell you about a couple of my earliest experiences as an interview subject: one when I was prepared, the other when I was not. The very first time a newspaper reporter interviewed me was in 1960. The reporter who did the interview was Ed Klein, who became famous later on as the editor of the *New York Times Magazine*, a *Vanity Fair* editor, and as the author of two very controversial books about Hillary Rodham Clinton. All that was in the future; at the time he interviewed me Ed was a reporter for the now-defunct *New York World-Telegram and The Sun*. He was assigned to interview me because I had recently been arrested, interrogated, and expelled from the Soviet Union for, in the words of a Moscow police document, "forcing noxious propaganda on unwilling Soviet citizens." (Actually, the Muscovites had been clamoring for copies of a U.S. State Department exchange magazine called *Amerika*.). After interviewing me, Ed wrote a long, complete story filled with direct quotes. It was, as they say in the trade, "a good yarn" — American college kid caught up in the cold war superpower confrontation, busted on the streets of the Soviet capital, sloppily and ineptly interrogated, and finally tossed out of the country in an exhibition of bureaucratic fumbling worthy of the Keystone Kops. I was very pleased with the piece; it accurately described my adventure and reflected what I said, often using my own words to tell the story.

It was not until years later that I would again be interviewed. Over those years, I went on to earn a degree from the Columbia University Graduate School of Journalism, I became a reporter at the very same *World-Telegram and The Sun* where Ed Klein had worked, and then I became a network television news producer at ABC. In all, about ten years passed between that first interview and my next one. Now over the course of that decade, I conducted hundreds of interviews myself, so you would think I would be prepared when it was once again my turn as an interview subject. Given my journalism career, I was pretty cocky about the interview. Of all people, *I* certainly knew what to do in an interview. This was going to be easy. The interview was with a New York Daily News TV page reporter and was conducted over the phone. I was very much at ease; too at ease, as you'll see. Our conversation was brief, friendly, and casual. And yet the next day, when I read the few paragraphs the reporter had written, I found them to be oddly unsatisfying. There were no quotes; the reporter had paraphrased what I had said.

I had failed to express myself in a quoteworthy manner; nothing I'd said warranted a direct quote; I had been neither concise, witty, nor specific enough to earn myself the medal of quotation marks around my own words. That was strange to me because, as a reporter, I was always on the lookout for good quotes for my own stories. Ten years earlier, talking to Ed Klein, I had given him a lot of good quotes. Looking back on that earlier experience, I realized I had been entertaining as well as informative with Ed; I had helped him with that good yarn. The second time around, I contributed nothing beyond basic, factual answers. I made no effort to excite or entertain a reader; I was, sin of all sins, dull! I could — and should — have illustrated my answers with anecdotes and engaging metaphors. Instead, I just answered the questions as if I had been on the witness stand in court — with barely more than "yes" and "no" responses.

The story limply sat on the page, drab as a dirty, old mop. I had failed to give the reporter good material to work with; I'd been unprepared. Which brings us to:

COMMANDMENT 1:
THOU SHALT BE PREPARED

What was the difference between those two interviews? In the first I had a good story to tell; an adventure to relate — my arrest and interrogation by the Soviet police, my expulsion from the country, and my hero's welcome in Poland where, despite the Communist government, anything that smacked of anti-Soviet or anti-Russian behavior won applause from the people. Also, I had agenda points to serve: I felt my adventure dramatically illustrated the freedom-smothering effect of life in a totalitarian police state and it showed that the ancient animosities of Eastern Europe continued to smolder even under supposedly like-minded Communist regimes. Additionally, I prepared for that interview, albeit unintentionally. I had told friends and family the story many times since my return. With each telling, I refined it, making it a breezier, sometimes dramatic, sometimes humorous story. When I was answering Ed Klein's questions, I used the same lines that had been most effective in my earlier tellings of the tale. I could not know it at the time, but my refinement of the story by frequently retelling it, prepared me to give a good interview.

In contrast, before my second interview, I gave no forethought to what I would say or how I would say it; I'd been a passive and not at all creative participant with no real story of my own to relate. I had no agenda to press in the second interview; I had no message to get out. I merely serviced the reporter's agenda, which was to learn a few facts about a developing situation at ABC News. And I served that agenda poorly because I wasn't quotable. It was a classic missed opportunity.

Yes, an *opportunity*. Every interview is an opportunity; an opportunity to air your agenda. Of course, to do that you must have an agenda. Remembering my missed opportunity in that second interview and in the spirit of "do as I say, not as I did," implant this in your mind: Every time you are interviewed, you should have a prepared story, a point of view, a message, or a series of messages. To go into an interview unprepared, as I did, without an agenda of your own, is to blow a singular opportunity. Unless you are a movie star or hold a high public office, interview opportunities don't arrive every day. In fact, for most of us, interviews are few and far between. If you know an interview is coming, prepare. In my case, it wasn't as if the Daily News columnist had sidled up to me at the local ABC watering hole and casually inquired, "What's new?" No, he had called me up, told me he was working on a story, and asked me if he could get some information from me. I even had to call him back, so there had been some prep time — which I did not use to my advantage. While I failed to seize that opportunity, I did learn a lesson, and I never made that mistake again.

AN INTERVIEW IS A PERFORMANCE

In the first chapter, I wrote that I have media trained everyone from rock stars to rocket scientists. When I am dealing with the rock stars, I always advise them to think of an interview not as a conversation but rather as a performance. Well, when you're in an interview, get in touch with your inner rock star and perform. What's true for Kelly Clarkson is true for you, too; your interview should be a performance.

I challenge all the entertainers I media train with this thought: "You wouldn't get up on a stage and begin singing without knowing what you're going to sing, would you? You know your music, your lyrics, your instrumentation, and your choreography. You rehearse your material." And the same holds true, I tell them, for an interview. They need to know and rehearse their material and then they need to perform it. Entertainment clients get that right away. For people in business, science, government, and public service, the idea of an interview as a performance may seem a little strange at first. But that changes once I ask them if they have ever prepared for a speech or presentation by writing their remarks and then silently reading them at their desk or off their computer screen. If they have, it is inevitable that they have found — once the attention of an audience is on them — that there are phrases the eye skips over and the tongue trips over. Once you accept the notion that communicating effectively requires performing skills, you appreciate the compelling need for knowing your "lyrics," polishing your techniques, and rehearsing your moves.

Of course, I am not suggesting that rocket scientists — or anyone else for that matter — sing and dance for reporters (although that might supply the "fun" element the media love so much). But to make the most of any media opportunity, these clients — and you — need to have an agenda to "perform." In other words, "Thou Shalt Be Prepared."

POSITIVE MESSAGES (AGENDA POINTS)

The first step in fulfilling that preparedness commandment is to formulate an agenda. That agenda should be composed of what I call Positive Message Statements, or "the good PMS." Good PMS? I'll bet that got your attention. And, in fact, that's why I used Positive Message Statements and not some other term like positive message points or positive agenda messages; I wanted initials you would remember, hence Positive Message Statements or PMSs. These are the points you feel you must make during the interview. Although I use the word *positive*, not every message you deliver must wear a big happy face. Your PMSs could be health warnings, attacks on a political foe's policies, or pieces of crucial, but downbeat, information. For example, not too long ago I saw a public health official interviewed on one of the cable news channels. He was talking about influenza killing more Americans each year than AIDs. This was far from a happy face message point, but for his purposes it was a *Positive Message Statement* because his agenda was to convince more people in the highest risk groups— the elderly and those with compromised immune systems — to get an annual flu vaccination.

Now if you're going to follow that first commandment, Thou Shalt Be Prepared, you cannot leave your PMSs to chance. Instead, after giving serious consideration to what messages you want to get out, write them down ahead of time. If you're wondering how many agenda points are ideal for a typical interview, I advise clients never to go into an interview with fewer than three nor more than five. In the Appendix of this book is a worksheet for creating PMSs. I recommend using the printed worksheet as a guide and doing the actual agenda-building on worksheets you create on your computer. That's because the work is easier to save and revise in a computer. But regardless of whether you do your agenda on a computer or write it out in pencil on the back of a number ten envelope, before every interview, fill out a new worksheet. If you do this, you'll find that your message points evolve, develop, and grow as you do more interviews. So going through the step of writing out your PMSs anew before each interview is not an exercise in repetition, it is an aid to enhancing and polishing them.

KNOW WHAT'S GOING ON IN YOUR WORLD

Your job in an interview is to give information to the reporter, not to learn information from the reporter. If your interviewer knows more about you, your company, your project, your product or your field of expertise than you do, your credibility is seriously compromised. To avoid that happening, as close to the time of an interview as possible, go to Google News (https://news.google.com) and in the search box type key words about your organization and your subject. Even the least prepared reporter will have done that basic bit of research. You want to know what the reporter is likely to know.

A dramatic case in point: I was doing a media training workshop for a government agency and just before the session began I typed the name of the agency into Google News. Up popped a story that a high-ranking administrator in the agency had resigned minutes earlier. During the first practice interview with group, I asked the participant about the resignation. He'd heard nothing about it and was stunned by the question. His reaction was classic deer-in-the-headlights bewilderment. It was a perfect teachable moment. You can bet that no one who participated in that workshop ever went into an interview without checking Google News. In addition to Google News, you should also check speciality news sources that deal with your area of expertise or authority. And, if you're involved in a controversy, check the web sites of your opponents; you want to know what they are saying about your side so you can respond.

So being prepared has two components: having an agenda and knowing what's going on in your world. But wait! Before you begin fashioning those PMSs, you need to pay heed to the second commandment:

COMMANDMENT 2:
THOU SHALT KNOW THY LISTENER

This second Boy Scout or "Be Prepared" Commandment probably has you asking yourself, "Is this guy kidding?" Of course you know your listener; you are speaking to a reporter. Maybe it's a reporter for *Business Week*. Perhaps it's the writer/editor/publisher of your local neighborhood weekly. It could be

Matt Lauer on "The Today Show." Or maybe it's the deep-voiced reporter for the local all-news radio station. In each case, you're talking to an interviewer, right?

Wrong! You are never talking *to* an interviewer or a reporter; instead you are talking *through* the reporter, to his readers, viewers, or listeners. It's important to plant this fact firmly in your mind before creating your agenda points because the reporter is likely to be better-informed, far more knowledgeable, and even more interested in what you have to say than his audience will be. In fact, some reporters, especially on science, political, business and technology beats, like to show off their knowledge to their interview subjects, and that display of reportorial sophistication may lull you into communicating at a level that's out of reach of your real audience: the reporter's readers, viewers, or listeners.

During my seven years at "Good Morning America," ABC's Entertainment Division controlled the show. In the early days, ABC News executives registered loud and frequent complaints about "show biz" people interviewing newsmakers, such as politicians and statesmen. The Entertainment Division yielded to the news executives' complaints, and ordered us to include a news correspondent in any interview with a guest who might make news. Although I came out of news and, in fact, had been plucked from the ranks of ABC News to be a producer at "Good Morning America," I quickly developed my own gripe, directed at those news correspondents forced into our interviews. My problem with the journalists was that they frequently phrased their questions to newsmaker guests with the assumption that the viewer knew as much as the interviewer. Because these reporters knew the inside stuff and all the arcane background of a story, they based their questions on that knowledge. It was often knowledge most viewers didn't share. It was exclusionary questioning, and too often the answers were equally exclusionary, our guests being only too happy to reply at the level of sophistication of the questioner rather than at the level of sophistication of the viewer. I can't tell you how many times I rolled my eyes in frustration when an ABC News correspondent launched into a complex question about the intricacies of, say, U.N. Resolution 242, without explaining to the viewers what Resolution 242 was. If, as was often the case, our guest replied in equally inaccessible language, it fell to our layman or non-journalist host, David

Hartman, to waste valuable air time backing up and filling in the blanks in the viewer's knowledge.

Before he began hosting "Good Morning America," Hartman had been an actor. He never attended journalism school nor did he work as a newsman. But he was an instinctive interviewer and one of his greatest strengths was his gift for asking questions viewers wanted answered; questions phrased in language viewers could comprehend. David did not ask questions designed to show off how much he knew.

Some TV critics and more than a few colleagues at ABC News initially belittled David's common man touch, but audiences responded in droves, and within a year of its creation, the upstart "Good Morning America" was solidly beating the long-established "Today Show" in the ratings. That trouncing continued for about a decade until "Today" acquired a production staff and cast that realized viewers wanted information in understandable language, not showoff presenters who were eager to leave viewers in the dust of confusion.

IDENTIFYING YOUR AUDIENCE AND YOUR INTERVIEWER'S AGENDA

How do you go about tailoring the tone and language of your messages to meet the wants and needs of your interviewer's audience? First of all, you need to determine who is in that audience. That's the easiest part of this second preparedness commandment.

All you have to do is read the reporter's publication, listen to her radio station, or watch his television program, and you will be able to determine its target audience. You will want to speak differently to a reader of *Aviation Week* or *Barron's* than you will to the more general audience reading *USA Today* or watching "Good Morning America." Your first job is to analyze whom the outlet appeals to.Your second job is to gauge how it engineers that appeal. In other words, does it seek a mass audience by shocking, angering, or frightening them? (Remember the first two of our "f" words: Fear and Fury?) Or does it appeal to the same audience by entertaining them?   (Another of our "f" words: Fun.) Does it look for an audience of sophisticated experts and engage them by offering detailed and solid information? Or is it a purveyor of general information for a mass audience?   You'll need to know so you can gear your level up or down to meet the audience's needs.

If at all possible, watch, listen to, or read the work of the individual reporter scheduled to interview you, and take comprehensive notes on your observations. If it's going to be a print interview, read any bylined pieces so you have an idea of whether she comes to the job with a specific attitude or special knowledge. If it's a broadcast, see what tone he adopts with his interview subjects — is he friendly and cooperative or challenging and prosecutorial? You can't change the reporter's manner, but you can prepare yourself so his attitude doesn't surprise you when you face him on camera. The late Mike Wallace, the attack bulldog of "60 Minutes" was a guest on the CBS program "The Early Show" in January, 2003, and Harry Smith asked him why, knowing his reputation for dogged questioning, people with something to hide submitted to his interviews. It was a good question because anyone who's watched even a modicum of television over the 30 years preceding that interview knew who Wallace was and what he did in an interview. Wallace answered, "I don't know. Maybe the bad guys don't think they're really in the fraternity until they've been exposed on '60 Minutes.'"

Mike Wallace was known nationally and his interview tactics were no secret. His role as prosecutorial interrogator at "60 Minutes" has been assumed by Steve Kroft and Leslie Stahl and across the country other interviewers serve his legacy. This requires you to do some homework in order to prepare. Familiarize yourself with your interviewer's work. If he is someone who's free to express opinions — like a columnist —try to gauge his position vis-à-vis your messages. Does the reporter, the publication, or the broadcast have a point of view? What is the outlet looking for: facts, fury, or fun? Is it accurate and factual or lurid and sensational? Do your research and you will be able to avoid surprises. Over the last several years, reporters have gotten increasing license to inject their attitudes into the news — especially on television. ABC News, which strives to be seen as nonpartisan, tolerated — perhaps even encouraged — John Stossel's antigovernment, libertarian and contrarian views on "20/20," which he co-anchored. Now he has found a home at Fox News. CNN made promotional capital of Lou Dobbs' crusades against outsourcing and illegal immigration and it happily touts Nancy Grace's hard-line approach to crime and criminal suspects. Fox News is home to a large roster of conservative partisan pundits in its anchor and reporting staff and MSNBC serves the other side of the political spectrum. By doing your research in advance, you'll know what you're getting into.

Speaking of surprises, I can recall a stunning example from the early days of "Good Morning America." Back then, we staged a daily six or seven minute debate that we called "Face Off." We would select a hot topic and, with David Hartman moderating, we would have representatives of opposing points of view argue about it. The goal was to shed some light and maybe a little entertaining heat on a subject that viewers would find important. One such "Face Off" featured Ron Kovic, the Marine Corps Vietnam veteran whose combat wounds left him paralyzed and wheelchair-bound. Kovic wrote about the experience in the extraordinary and passionate antiwar book, *Born on the Forth of July.* The subject was government truthfulness, or lack of truthfulness, during times of war. Kovic's adversary was Gen. William Westmoreland, the retired former commander of U.S. forces in Vietnam. Normally on "Good Morning America" we preinterviewed our guests. For our "Face Offs" these preinterviews were essential lest we find on the air that the guests agreed with each other. Gen. Westmoreland would not make himself available for the preinterview, but since we knew he and Kovic disagreed, we went ahead with the segment. Had the general submitted to the preinterview, he might have learned about the passion and intensity of his opponent. In addition to not submitting to a preinterview, it was clear that the general had not read nor read about Kovic's bestselling book. Hard as it may be to believe, Westmoreland seemed not to know that the intense, longhaired and bearded man he faced was a furious antiwar activist. I sensed the general thought he was sitting down to a gentlemanly discussion, so he was unprepared for the passionate attack Kovic launched. The encounter left the surprised Westmoreland almost speechless, stunned by Kovic's verbal assault. Just a little preparation would have enabled Gen. Westmoreland to put up his guard and get in his points. But he had not prepared and Kovic pummeled him like a heavyweight pro taking on a lightweight amateur. The best way to avoid an on-air pummeling is to do your homework before sitting down for the interview or the broadcast; you need to know as much as possible about both the reporter and about anyone else he will interview for the story.

How Are Stories Built?

When you are reviewing the publication or broadcast that is sending a reporter to interview you, pay special attention to how it uses quotes . For print media, does the publication write stories by stringing together quotes with little interpretive continuity from the writer? Or is it largely writer opinion and observation illustrated by an occasional, brief quote? In electronic media, do the soundbites run short or long? Analytical viewing will show you that the half-hour network newscasts run very short soundbites while the magazine shows like "60 Minutes," "20/20," "48 Hours," and "Dateline NBC" run longer soundbites. If you know the style of the publication or broadcast, you can phrase your answers so they get maximum play.

When you do this you help yourself by tailoring your responses to the medium, making it more likely the outlet will use your words. And you help the reporter by making his job easier, supplying him with quotes and eliminating his need to paraphrase you. If the publication or broadcast uses extensive, technically detailed quotes, providing that detail in your answers helps the reporter write his story accurately. Conversely, if the outlet goes for the "common touch" and you express yourself accordingly, the reporter is more likely to use your direct quotes and not have to work hard simplifying what you said so his readers can understand it. Remember, the more a reporter paraphrases you, the more opportunity there is for your points to lose focus. Reporters want to quote you rather than paraphrase you, but you need to give them the wherewithal to do that.

Crafting Your Messages
for Your Audience

Once you have identified your audience and your interviewer's likely agenda, you are ready to craft your messages. Think of what you want that audience to know about your program, company, idea, or product and then use the worksheet in the appendix, or one you create yourself, to write out the messages you want the audience to take away from the finished story. When you're done with your worksheet, take as much time as you need to read your message statements aloud at least twice and think about them with as much detachment as you can muster. They are, after all, your Positive Message Statements. You created them in your self-interest, but you want your audience to be receptive to them. So, the first question to ask yourself is, "Do my messages sound like someone speaking or do they sound too 'literary?'" If the answer is too literary, you're probably writing for the eye not the ear. That is, you're writing something that is more easily absorbed when read than when heard. You want to redraft your agenda points so that they are more conversational. The second question to ask yourself is, "Do they sound like slogans, commercials, or sermons?" If so, that's probably because you wrote them exclusively from your point of view. Instead, you should adopt the point of view of your ultimate audience. To identify with that audience, think of a radio station whose call-letters are WSIC. Whether your audience is watching your interview on TV, reading an account of it in a magazine, or listening to you on radio, its members have at least this one thing in common: they are all simultaneously listening to WSIC. Whether your audience is the broad-based readership of *USA Today* or the scientists and science-obsessed who subscribe to the journal *Science*, they are all listening to WSIC. The call-letters stand for:

WSIC

W — Why
S — Should
I
C — Care

Everyone you are trying to reach with your messages is subconsciously wondering why those messages should concern him or how those messages affect him. Remember what I wrote earlier about David Hartman seizing the morning ratings lead by asking the questions viewers wanted answered? Well that works both ways — for the interviewee as well as for the interviewer. You won't always be fortunate enough to have a David Hartmanesque interviewer, one who is seeking information for his viewers. Sometimes your interviewer will be too rushed, too overwhelmed, too indifferent, too expert, or too egotistical to care about the audience. So it's incumbent on you to care. You need to broaden your messages so your real audience understands why it should care about them. You need to tell people what's in it for them.

Previously, I wrote about the interview with the public health official who talked about influenza killing more Americans each year than AIDs. In a case like that it's pretty self-evident why a listener or reader should care. The information is a matter of life and death. The WSIC challenge is much greater when you are trying to deliver messages that don't concern life or death issues. How do you make someone care if you're the spokesperson for a rock band or an orbiting telescope? What if your interview goal is to promote a new candy bar or a soft drink? You need to step outside your spokesperson's role and ask yourself what it is about your messages would interest you if you were *not* the spokesperson. What about your messages would interest your Aunt Matilda and Uncle Joe? There's always something; your job is to find it. People respond to a good story, to being entertained, to the opportunity to pursue pleasure, and to advice that enables them to avoid the unpleasant. These are not life or death matters like the flu, but they are reason enough to absorb and remember your messages. It is your job to make those connections.

Using the copy of the agenda worksheet from the appendix — or the worksheet you created on your computer — rework and fine-tune your PMSs for the WSIC listeners. When you're finished reread them aloud again and then write down specifically how you've answered the WSIC question. Your WSIC response can be just a word or two, like "saves you money," "entertaining," "promotes education," "stimulates the imagination."

BUT WAIT, THERE'S MORE....

Commandments 1 and 2, Thou Shalt Be Prepared and Thou Shalt Know Thy Listener, are important rules for a successful interview.

Knowing before the interview ever begins what you want to say and to whom you'll be saying it is more than half the preparation battle. In fact, having an agenda in advance is the single most important step in preparing for an interview. While those two commandments are the top of the Be Prepared list, there are some additional steps that are vital in helping you be the best prepared, most articulate and effective interview subject you can be.

ADDITIONAL PREPARATION TIPS

Arrive Early
Warm Up
Be Discreet
Eat Something
Don't Assume you Have Friends in the Media
Leave Comedy to the Comedians

¶ **Arrive early.** On the morning of Ronald Reagan's first inauguration, January 21, 1981, we were broadcasting "Good Morning America" from a temporary studio built atop a high scaffold overlooking the White House. Our first guest for the day, in our 7:00-7:30 half-hour, was Sen. Barry Goldwater. At about 5:30 in the morning, as technicians were still doing last minute checks of gear and David Hartman and the producers were beginning to do a final read-through of the script, one of our staffers burst into the studio and said, "Senator Goldwater's here. He's climbing the stairs." The stairs in this case went three stories straight up without any landings for catching your breath. The senator had recently undergone hip surgery, so I ran out to intercept him before he climbed all those steps. I wanted to tell him that he was extremely early and might be more comfortable waiting at street level. I was too late; when I got to him he was already more than halfway up the stairs.

"Oh, it's O.K.," he said. "I always arrive early." "We don't have a Green Room up there," I said. "I'll sit in the corner and read the papers." Under his arm he was carrying several newspapers. Once inside the studio, he took a seat in the back and read the newspapers he had brought. Then the senator read the newspapers we had on hand and scanned the wire service copy. Finally — when we finished all our briefings — he talked informally with David Hartman and Steve Bell, the show's news anchor.

Sen. Goldwater, a media pro, arrived early for several good reasons. He was insuring he'd be on time, he'd be oriented to the interview's surroundings, he'd be informed (the newspapers and the wire service copy), and he could review his agenda in a leisurely way. Also, his early arrival gave him the opportunity for an advance chat with his interviewers.

Arriving early is especially important for broadcast interviews. There is nothing worse than rushing into a radio or television studio at the last minute, sitting down and trying to respond to that first question while you are panting like a sprinter, catching his breath after running 100 meters. Chances are good you'll be so harried you won't convey your messages effectively.

¶ **Warm up**. As Sen. Goldwater did, chat with the reporter before the interview. Consider it a mental stretching exercise or a warmup before your race. If it's a television interview, introduce yourself to the crew, too. Some TV reporters follow a rigid caste system and will not introduce you to these people, but don't let their rudeness stop you. The camera crew and lighting technicians can make you look good or bad and if you've taken the trouble to say hello to them, they'll treat you better than if you snub them. I remember Rosalynn Carter, former President Jimmy Carter's wife, doing that during the 1976 presidential campaign. Mrs. Carter was a guest on "Good Morning America." She took time during the commercial before her appearance to walk up to each cameraman, stagehand, and technician and introduce herself. When she sat down for that interview, there were ten people on the set who would have set things right if even a single hair on Mrs. Carter's head had been out of place. After the interview the future first lady made the rounds again and thanked each person on the set.

¶ **Be discreet.** It is very important when you're chatting up the cast and crew to avoid saying anything you don't want the entire world to know. ("Boy, is our company having a terrible quarter. I don't know if we can avoid bankruptcy. But you won't ask me about that, will you?") Of course you wouldn't do that, right? Well, don't be too sure. In a pre-interview warmup, I once heard an actress say, "You know, I won't talk about my relationship with X, so don't even bother asking." An early question in the interview was: "You've said you won't talk about your relationship with X. Well, why won't you talk about it?" She wasn't asked about the relationship; the reporter respected her wishes in a literal sense. But the question she actually got was a lot more damaging. So instead of talking about what you can't say, use the warmup for what you can say and want to say: your interview agenda.

Whenever you are in proximity to a journalist, you are being interviewed. A print reporter can hear a quote, remember it, and write it down after the fact and use it in her article. A broadcast correspondent can report on the air something you've said to her away from the microphone: "Off-camera Ms. Marmot told me that the Ynot Company is on the brink of bankruptcy...."

You may be asking yourself, "If there is such a big danger of being overly confidential, why bother with the stretch/warm-up before the interview?" The answer is that the benefits outweigh the risks; with just a little discipline you will be able to use this opportunity to plant the seeds of some of your agenda points in the reporter's mind, inviting questions that will elicit those points in formal the interview. So just as you have an agenda for the interview, you should have a Cliff Notes version of that agenda for the warmup as well.

Shortly before President Nixon's resignation in 1974, I produced a story called "The Business of Watergate" for the ABC News weekly magazine show, "The Reasoner Report." The story told how various Watergate figures were cashing in on their notoriety by writing books and giving lectures about the break-in and subsequent cover-up. I interviewed James McCord for the piece. One of the Watergate burglars, McCord had written a book called *A Piece of Tape*. While the crew set up the lights and camera in McCord's office in the Washington suburbs, he began talking to me about the break-in and gave a couple of details that I'd not heard or read before. So when the camera was rolling, I asked him about them. He repeated them — in the context of their being revealed for the first time in his book. We both went away happy. I had filmed some new pieces of the Watergate puzzle and McCord had a plug for his book. He had used his warmup time with me most effectively.

¶ **Eat something.** Picture this scene. On "Good Morning America," David Hartman has just introduced his guest, a prominent attorney. David asks her a question and she stammers for an answer. David asks her another question and instead of answering, she leans back in the chair and her eyes roll up. "Are you O.K.?" David asks. Unable to answer, her eyes closing, the attorney slowly shakes her head. David leans forward, takes her hand and began gently slapping her wrist to get her pulse going. We cut to a commercial.

As this dramatic scene unfolded live on camera, someone in the control room phoned 911 and an ambulance arrived quickly and whisked the guest to nearby Roosevelt Hospital.

Later in the day, she returned to the office to let the show's staff know she was O.K. She told me: "My mother always said breakfast was the most important meal of the day. She never told me *how* important." She had eaten nothing before the show, even though we stocked our Green Room with food. On the air, her blood sugar level dropped sharply, leaving her lightheaded and feeling faint. The stress of the interview environment may have exacerbated her problem.

Pay attention to what you eat before an interview. Physicians I've consulted on the subject recommend eating complex carbohydrates (like fruit) and avoiding processed sugars, which can make you lethargic. In fact, on the advice of Dr. Tim Johnson, "Good Morning America's" on-camera medical editor, we stocked our Green Room with an ample supply of fresh fruit and a vegetable platter with a low-fat dip in addition to the traditional sticky buns, bagels and sugared pastries. Avoid alcoholic beverages before an interview; their "calming" qualities are not worth the risk. I've seen more than a few interview subjects show up drunk and slur their way through a conversation with a reporter. In the most extreme case in my career, a famous college football coach was so drunk during a live interview he wet himself and was unaware of it until he got up to leave the set. In addition to booze, avoid carbonated beverages. You don't want to be sitting on camera or in front of a radio microphone stifling belches.

¶ **Don't assume you have friends in the media.**

¶ **Leave comedy to the comedians.** I've lumped these two together because comedienne Tina Fey has been kind enough to supply us with a teachable moment by violating both points as well as our earlier tip — **Be Discreet**. The lesson is in her best-selling memoir, "Bossypants." In 2008, while the Obama-McCain election campaign was in full swing, *TV Guide* assigned Damian Holbrook to do a profile of Tina. This was great news for Fey; she and Holbrook were old friends. Lulled into thinking Holbrook was a friend first and a journalist second, Fey violated the other two caveats.

Here's her account: "Long after what I considered the 'interview portion' of our day to be over, Damian asked me what I would do if McCain-Palin won the election. Would I continue to moonlight at SNL (Saturday Night Live)? I said in a jokey, actress-y voice, 'If they win, I will leave Earth.' It was clearly a joke about people who say stupid things like that. No matter what your political beliefs, everyone knows some loudmouth: 'If Bush wins, I'm moving to Canada.' 'If Bush wins again, I am seriously moving to Canada.'

"But Damian put 'I'm leaving Earth' in his article, and in print it looked sincerely idiotic.... I looked like a grade A dummy. I was annoyed at Damian, but mostly I just found it disconcerting. That I could get in 'trouble' for a half-baked joke I made in my own home was a level of scrutiny I did not enjoy."

Fey said something in front of a reporter that she didn't want the whole world to read and the whole world wound up reading it.

Another case history: in 2010, General Stanley McChrystal — on his way to Washington where President Obama was planning to turn over to him overall control of the Afghanistan war — stopped at a bar in Germany with his staff. There, the officers engaged in a lot of disparaging conversation about their civilian bosses. They did it in front of Rolling Stone's Michael Hastings who did what journalists do when they hear news: he reported it. It's likely McChrystal and his staff thought they were speaking in front of a friend because Hastings had been embedded with U.S. troops in Afghanistan. They were wrong; McChrystal lost his job and resigned from the Army.

Following Commandments 1 and 2 will prepare and empower you to make your points in any interview. By creating your own agenda you'll gain confidence and avoid the disappointment of missed media opportunities. Knowing what you will and won't say are fundamental to media mastery. Your overall effectiveness as a spokesperson depends on having an agenda of messages that you want the reporter's audience to absorb and making those messages as relevant as possible. You also must express those messages effectively. Now let's move on to the commandments that will help you make your message presentation effective, commandments 3, 4 and 5; what I call the performance commandments.

CHAPTER 3

THE PERFORMANCE COMMANDMENTS

In the previous chapter I dealt with the first two commandments, the preparation commandments; the rules you follow for formulating your agenda and for preparing to deliver it. The next three commandments deal with that delivery. I call them the performance commandments, because — as I wrote — you should always think of an interview as a performance. Obeying these commandments will make you a better performer:

THE PERFORMANCE COMMANDMENTS

III. Thou shalt be quoteworthy.
IV. Thou shalt practice, practice, practice.
V. Thou shalt not lie, evade, speculate, nor cop an attitude.

Marshall McLuhan, widely celebrated as the "oracle of the electronic age," wrote a book called *The Medium is the Massage*, which is almost universally misread as *The Medium is the Message* (with an *e* rather than an *a)*. That misreading has licensed two generations of spokespersons to think that merely getting their face on television or their name in print is the equivalent of successfully delivering their message. But pay close attention to the exact spelling McLuhan used: the title is a play on words; McLuhan wrote m*a*ssage, not m*e*ssage. The word play cleverly conflates two meanings: "the medium is the *mass age*" or, the more literal: the medium *massages* our brains just as a masseuse kneads our muscles.

For our purposes, let's continue the popular misconstruction of his little pun, call it "m*e*ssage" but stand it on its head. For us, then, your *message* is the message and the *medium* is just that: the mechanism for delivering the message. In other words, the medium is *not* the message. But, with a nod of recognition to McLuhan's pun, the medium does require us to massage our message in order to express it most effectively. Each of the different media require that we slightly temper, alter, and tailor our message to accommodate its specific requirements. More on those unique aspects of the different media in succeeding chapters. But for now, let's concentrate on the universal rules for all media; rules which begin with the three performance commandments:

COMMANDMENT 3:
THOU SHALT BE QUOTEWORTHY

In the previous chapter I wrote how disappointed I was when I read the story that emerged from my chat with the *Daily News* reporter who interviewed me at ABC News. He used no direct quotes, but paraphrased my remarks and I felt I had been a dull and ineffective spokesperson. I failed to take advantage of the opportunity to get any messages to his readers because I had prepared no messages. I had no agenda; no Positive Message Statements to expound. And whatever expounding I had done in the service of *his* agenda had not been quoteworthy material. In broadcasting terms, I had not spoken in soundbites. After that second interview, I began paying extremely close attention to direct quotes in newspapers and magazine stories. I listened more analytically to television news reports, including those I, myself, produced. I had always been able to identify a good soundbite. But now I wanted to codify a formula for them. What, exactly, made them good? Until then I had been relying on instinct; I wanted to figure out if I could apply a set of rules to good quotes and soundbites.

What began as a casual investigation became a thirty-year study. To this day I never read a newspaper, listen to a radio newscast, or watch a TV news program without mentally grading the interview subjects.

Some get an F; they fail miserably. You can tell this group very quickly: usually, not a word of what they said is in direct quotes in a print story. If they are part of a television report, you may see them talking on camera but their words are muted and the correspondent is telling us what they said. This is because they have expressed themselves so badly their actual words are unusable.

The majority of interview subjects earn a mediocre C. There may be a direct quote from them in print, but most likely it's just a sentence or a sentence fragment. The C interview subject may get eight or nine seconds of a soundbite on television or radio, but often their statements aren't even complete sentences and the correspondent feels compelled to contribute a voiceover "intro" (introduction) to set up the bite or an "outro" (outroduction?) to clarify or amplify what the subject was trying to say.

A handful of interviewees earn an A. They are quoted profusely in print. In the electronic media whole sentences — indeed, whole paragraphs — run uninterrupted. They speak in short, comprehensible sentences and there are no ambiguities in their answers. They never equivocate or evade. Also, they use grabbers, word techniques that make an idea into a soundbite, verbal devices that give life to an idea. A little later, I'll show you how to create grabbers.

Aside from its appeal to our competitive instincts, why strive for an A in an interview? What's wrong with a comfortable C? For that matter, is it a crime to flunk? No, it's not a crime; you won't be left back, sent to detention, ordered to write an essay, or required to take a makeup test. But a failing grade means you have not communicated as effectively as you could; you've missed an opportunity to directly sell your ideas, company, product, or organization to a wide audience. Also, a C interview subject invites the reporter to paraphrase him. When a reporter paraphrases, the chances of misinterpretation and distortion increase.

The A interviewee is in control. He takes advantage of the opportunity interviews offer to reach large audiences with messages expressed in his own words. To a large extent C, and more so the D and F interviewees, miss out on that opportunity. They are not in control and depend on the reporter to help them convey ideas. The reporter may not accommodate them. Through ineptitude, indifference, or even malice, the reporter may misconstrue, misinterpret, or misstate the message. Many of my media training clients have told me that past interviewers "got it wrong," inaccurately conveying their messages. If you force the journalist to filter your ideas because you don't express them clearly, there is always the risk that the reporter's filter will distort what you say. An A interview subject keeps control by being *quoteworthy*.

To be quoteworthy you need to speak in soundbites. A soundbite is the mass media's most valuable commodity — a short, pithy, meaningful statement, a verbal headline.

SOUNDBITES

Critics deplore soundbite journalism as bad journalism. The soundbite, they charge, is the curse of television news; proof of the medium's superficiality. Most of those who make this charge are print reporters who often prove their point by citing television's critics in direct quotes which are suspiciously like soundbites. For example: "Soundbite journalism is infantile, puerile, and futile. It's like a souffle′ — all fluff and no substance." A good quote which, if lifted from the printed page and uttered on TV or radio, would be a good soundbite!

So what is a good soundbite? A brief statement that captures attention, delivers a message, and does it in a way that's sufficiently dramatic or witty to remain in an audience member's memory. Good soundbites can come from anyone. Reporting on a tornado that devastated a small Southern town, *The New York Times* quoted a fourth grader as saying, "The good news is we don't have school tomorrow. The bad news is we don't have a school."

Newspapers like *The New York Times* use soundbites all the time — they just call them direct quotes. Soundbites have been around forever, only the name is relatively new. Shakespeare's plays are full of lines that make fine soundbites ("Neither a borrower nor a lender be."). And so is the Bible ("The wages of sin is death."). Soundbites aren't just the currency of literature and religion; every great line we remember from our history courses qualifies as a soundbite. Here are some classics:

"Give me liberty or give me death."
- Patrick Henry (1775)

"Here I stand; I can do no otherwise."
- Martin Luther (1521)

"It's a recession when your neighbor loses his job; it's a depression when you lose yours."
- Harry Truman (1956)

Two of those soundbites predate television news and all electronic media. In fact, Luther's predates the first serious study of electricity by sixty years. Soundbites are the currency of history, and journalism is history's first draft.

Here's a little homework assignment: next time you're reading a newspaper or magazine, compare how much text in a story is within quotation marks with how much is not. When you read the directly quoted material, assess the amount and quality of information in those quotes. Ordinarily, the direct quotes will share two attributes: good solid, comprehensible information and a deft turn of phrase. You can find direct quotes in which only one or another of those attributes will be present, but in those cases, you will notice that it's more likely that a deft turn of language is directly quoted than an inelegantly phrased, information-filled sentence. Reporters will paraphrase information, rather than force readers to deconstruct a meandering quote.

The New York Times celebrates the best daily soundbite in its Quote of the Day. Over the course of a month I kept careful score of the Quote of the Day and during that period the average length of the quote/soundbite was under 20 words. Most were no more than two sentences and some were as short as a single sentence of as few as 10 words. We'll deal with the ideal construction and length of soundbites a little later on and you'll learn exactly how to express your agenda in compelling soundbites. Many newspapers highlight important quotes by printing them in boldface and enclosing them in a box within the body of a news story. These are called "pull quotes."

PERFECTING A SOUNDBITE

Looking back at such masters of soundbites as Shakespeare, John F. Kennedy, Harry Truman, Patrick Henry, Ronald Reagan, Winston Churchill, and others we can see that there is nothing intrinsically wrong with answering a question with a soundbite, especially if the soundbite serves your purpose by vividly illustrating your message. Soundbite journalism gets a bad rap, many consider it "short shrift" journalism — superficial reporting and writing. And, in fact, many soundbites *are* bad, amounting to little more than slogans, conveying scant substance. This is not necessarily because the interviewee doesn't know his area of expertise. The more likely explanation is he did not have the skill set to make the most out of his media opportunity.

SOUNDBITES FOR YOUR
AGENDA POINTS

In the last chapter, you created an agenda of three to five Positive Message Statements. That is the first step in producing good soundbites. Your PMSs are the basis for your interview; expressing them in soundbites will bring your agenda to life, and make it compelling to the media. Remember my three pigeon holes for answers from the first chapter? Can't use that; could use that; gotta use that? Now let's revisit your messages and turn them into *gotta use that* soundbites.

First you need to hone your PMSs so they have fine, sparkling, razor-like edges. Next, you'll need to deliver them in an assertive, positive manner without temporizing, compromising, or stumbling. If that sounds daunting, it can be, but only if you don't take the time to prepare. As I wrote earlier, an interview is a performance and the benefits of preparing for that performance are worth the effort. A key part of that preparation is working on your soundbites in advance of every interview; making them sharp enough to cut through the fog.

The historical soundbites on page 38 are uniformly direct, concise, and bold. And short. The longest soundbite I quoted was Harry Truman's line about the difference between a recession and a depression. It's a mere 16 words long. Compare his line with a less effective alternate that expresses the same idea:

Truman: "It's a recession when your neighbor loses his job; it's a depression when you lose yours."

Alternate: "It's a recession when your neighbor is out of work; it's a depression when you are."

The difference is that Truman's soundbite is in the active voice, the alternative is in the passive voice: "loses his job" versus "is out of work." The active verb *loses* is more powerful than the passive *is out of work*. So use the active voice.

Here is a soundbite from President Franklin D. Roosevelt: "The only thing we have to fear is fear itself." It is only ten words long. (It is misquoted frequently in eight words: "We have nothing to fear but fear itself.") The Roosevelt quote is from his first inaugural address, so it was less off-the-cuff than the Truman recession/depression line. It is also likely Roosevelt's memorable quote was the result of fine-tuning by accomplished speechwriters — FDR had successful poets and playwrights on his speechwriting staff. Some vintage soundbites came from prepared remarks, too, while others were spontaneous. But you need not hire speechwriters and poets to do this work, and you do not have to read your soundbites. In fact, in most face-to-face interviews it would be a mistake to read them. And you do not need Harry Truman's spontaneous wit to come up with them, either. It's a good idea to compose your soundbites in advance and when the occasion presents itself in the form of a question, deploy them from memory.

President Truman, in particular, had a gift for concise and telling off-the-cuff remarks, making him a master of the soundbite. He famously said, "If you can't stand the heat, stay out of the kitchen." Another of his favorites was "The buck stops here." He had a small plaque on his Oval Office desk that read, "The buck stops here." Compare Truman's memorable line to similar sentiments expressed about 60 years later by President George W. Bush: "Presidents, whether things are good or bad, always get the blame." Both quotes have the same basic message, albeit Bush's is more defensive than Truman's. The language and active voice make Truman's memorable.

In my media training sessions, I urge participants not to memorize their entire answers, lest they sound overly rehearsed. But I make an exception for brief soundbites because, unless you've got Harry Truman's unique gift, you'd better plan, write, and rehearse these lines so they'll have maximum effect.

But, please, don't do as our current crop of politicians do and, upon finding a resonating soundbite, repeat it *ad nauseam* for the same audience. Remember Vice President Al Gore's "Social Security lockbox" in the 2000 presidential campaign? Or President Bush's "stay the course line" about the Iraq war? Both used their terms until they became grist for the mills of comedians. Patrick Henry didn't go around the colonies repeating "Give me liberty or give me death." He said it once in 1775 and it reverberates to this day.

In general, you can repeat a good soundbite until it becomes a cliché. At that point, let the media repeat it for you. Lockbox would have been O.K. on a Houston radio station then in a Denver newspaper and later in a TV newscast in Chicago. But after it was on the network nightly newscasts and in national media once or twice, Gore probably should have dropped it;

chances are good the media would have continued to use it for him.

COUNTERINTUITIVE COMMUNICATIONS

When we are talking through the media to the public we need to adopt some counterintuitive measures. Earlier I wrote that an interview is not a conversation, it is a performance. But we are more accustomed to having conversations than we are to performing. To be effective in an interview we must adopt some communications techniques that are counterintuitive to conversational exchanges.

AN ANSWER IS AN ISLAND

A conversation is an organic whole; it grows, flows and develops. My answers later on in a conversation will be understood because the other participants have been in the exchange from the beginning. But in an interview, only one or two of my answers may appear in the finished story, so I have to think of each answer as an island — able to stand on its own without reference to the question or anything I've said earlier. In a conversation, the listeners know the context of any answer I give. That's not true in a soundbite; the reader or listener in the audience does not know what was said earlier. Thus, "as I said," or "as you said" in an answer may render that answer unusable because the audience does not know what you said earlier. The audience may not even know the question if the reporter leaves it out of his story. (In broadcast journalism, reporters are loathe to use a bobbled question. If your answer is dependent on that question to be comprehensible, you are inviting the reporter not to use it.)

SPEAK IN COMPLETE SENTENCES;
INCLUDE THE SENSE OF THE QUESTION IN YOUR ANSWER

The easiest way to illustrate this point is to show you how to answer the most basic of questions. If I were to ask you, "What's the weather today?" an acceptable conversational answer would be, "It's sunny and warm and it's likely to remain that way all week." The question gives context to the response; I know — because I asked — that the "it" you are referring to is the weather. In an interview, our island answer should be, "The weather today is sunny and warm and it's likely to remain that way all week." The answer is a complete sentence that includes the sense of the question.

If you start an answer with the word "it's" or the word "because," you are having a conversation, not doing an interview. Banish pronouns from your interview answers. In a conversation, everyone knows what the "it" and who the "we" in your answer refers to; they have been present throughout the organic exchange. Though you may talk to a reporter for half an hour or more, only one or two of your answers will make it into the article or into the broadcast news story, so the audience does not have the same contextual understanding that a conversation participant has.

Delivering your answers in complete sentences enhances your control of the interview because the print reporter interviewing you won't have to add your missing words in brackets and the broadcast reporter won't have to write a tortured lead-in or lead-out to your soundbite. Since filling in your blanks or creating that tortured lead-in or lead-out is extra work, many reporters won't bother doing it; instead they will paraphrase your words — and you want to avoid being paraphrased.

The exception to the rule about including the sense of a question in your answer: never repeat the words or sense of a negative question. You may have read this quote in a news story: "This is not a disaster waiting to happen." I can guarantee it came in answer to this question: "Isn't this a disaster waiting to happen?" The correct response to "Isn't this a disaster waiting to happen?" is "No, it is not." This forces the reporter to use his question if he wants the word disaster to be heard or read. For an object lesson in what not to do, see the headline below:

That's the October 31, 2013 front page of the Los Angeles Times and the banner headline is quoting Secretary of Health and Human Services Kathleen Sebelius who was lured into using the D-word by Representative Marsha Blackburn, a Republican from Tennessee using a reporter's age-old trick question. And while Ms. Sebelius fell for it in a Congressional hearing, not a media interview, the lesson is still valid. (The fact is, many Congressional hearings are media events first and fact-finding ventures second.) Here is the exchange that led to the Los Angeles Times headline:

Blackburn: "Michelle Snyder is the one responsible for this debacle?" [Ms. Snyder was the chief operating officer at the Centers for Medicare & Medicaid.]

Sebelius: "Excuse me, congresswoman, Michelle Snyder is not responsible for the debacle. Hold me accountable for the debacle. I'm responsible."

Secretary Sebelius used Rep. Blackburn's negative word *twice* in two sentences! Had the secretary responded, "No, congresswoman, hold me responsible," any media outlet wanting to use the word "debacle" would have been forced to quote the representative. As it was, more than a few outlets, including the Los Angeles Times, used the answer without the question so that it appeared in the story that "debacle" was Secretary Sebelius' characterization. CBS News, on the other hand, used the soundbite, but showed Rep. Blackburn's maneuvering Secretary Sebelius into repeating the negative word.

Earlier, I urged you to be concise and bold with your soundbites. You *can* be too bold. Many years ago I covered a news conference by the leader of the Brooklyn longshoreman's union, the elderly but still combative Anthony "Tough Tony" Anastasio. A strike was looming and, on this particular day, Tough Tony, who looked like a grandfather but talked like the Godfather, told the assembled reporters that if there was not a new contract soon, "The docks is gonna run red wit' blood." His glib and polished second-in-command, Tony Scotto, who was also Tough Tony's son-in-law, quickly interjected: "What Pop means is…."

Tough Tony's soundbite probably played well with his restive union membership, but everyone else who heard it was appalled at his naked threat of violence. When making bold statements, you have to assess how they will play not only to the general public but also to specific audiences within the public. In a July, 2003 news conference, President Bush said of the Iraqi insurgency, which was in its early stages: "There are some who feel like that the conditions are such they can attack us there. My answer is bring 'em on." As Bush left the podium after the news conference, his press secretary, Ari Fleischer, privately told the chief executive that he took exception to the "bring 'em on" line because the families of soldiers serving in Iraq might find it offensive and insensitive. The statement struck more than just military families as being insensitive and next day, Fleischer was doing a Tony Scotto to Bush's Tough Tony Anastasio, telling reporters that the president had not meant to invite attacks on American troops: "I think what the president was expressing there is his confidence in the men and women of the military to handle the military mission." Four and a half years later, Scott Pelley of "60 Minutes" asked Bush what mistakes he had made in the Iraq war, and the president answered, "Abu Ghraib was a mistake. Using bad language like, you know, 'bring 'em on' was a mistake." Here was the president ranking a poorly-worded soundbite with the prisoner torture scandal. Do you need any further proof of how important soundbites are?

MORE QUOTEWORTHINESS TIPS

Here are some additional tips to help you obey the quoteworthiness commandment and turn your messages into *gotta use that* soundbites. Following these tips will make your broadcast soundbites and printed quotes more effective and memorable. I illustrate them with radio station call-letters:

THE SOUNDBITE RADIO STATIONS

KPUF: Key Point Up Front
KISS: Keep it Short and Simple
KOTJ: Knock off the Jargon

¶ **KPUF: Key Point Up Front.** In a conversation we usually build to a conclusion. We begin with a premise, add points and come to a conclusion. When we are talking to the public through interviews, we need to copy the media's technique and speak the way the media write: conclusion first, supporting data later. Read a news story or listen to a newscast and pay special attention to how writers structure the stories. Typically, there is a headline, then a lead sentence, and then supporting facts. (Broadcast reports often omit the headline, although an introductory line like, "Here's a frightening story from the Centers for Disease Control," is a verbal headline.) The lead sentence is the one that contains the most important information the reporter wishes to convey.

For most of us, it is counterintuitive to express ourselves this way, but there are valid reasons for doing it in interviews. In electronic media the listener or viewer doesn't have the advantage that a newspaper or magazine reader has — the ability to go back and revisit a line or a paragraph. I call this the reread factor. So in broadcast interviews it is vital that you get the most important elements up front to set the audience's mental agenda. I recommend doing this in print interviews as well, because you'll be speaking to the reporter exactly the way he writes his stories. Speaking this way makes it much more likely you'll wind up in direct quotes and not paraphrases. As a former print reporter, I can attest that my notes were always extremely legible at the start of a response and became more difficult to read as the answer progressed. Get your agenda point out before writer's cramp sets in.

¶ **KISS: Keep it Short and Simple**. Why short? Because if you go on and on and on and on and on and on and on and …. Get the point? If you are long-winded in a broadcast interview, you're going to lose your listener's interest and she'll forget how you started. In a print interview the listener who's going to lose interest is the reporter, and you don't want that. Why simple? Because if your answer gets too complicated, its WSIC (why should I care?) quotient dwindles. In media training workshops clients always ask me, "How short and how simple?" I answer by using social science research done by Vincent Covello, PhD., who has worked on these questions at Columbia University and at the National Research Council/National Academy of Sciences.

How simple? Remember the second commandment: Thou shalt know thy Listener? If your interview is with *USA Today*, "CBS This Morning," or "The Tonight Show," you're reaching a less sophisticated audience than if the interview is with the journal *Science* or *Barron's* or *Aviation Week.* For those specialized publications you can hike the sophistication level of your answers to match that of your audience. But for the mass-market media, use answers that are comprehensible at the U.S. national average grade level: the education grade level reached by the average citizen. In the United States, that's the tenth grade. In other words, you are talking to a fifteen- or sixteen-year-old. But here's a caveat: For emotion-charged stories where fear and fury reign, Dr. Covello's research dictates dropping down *four* grade levels. In other words, if you are talking about building a nuclear power plant down the street from a hospital, you'll need to make your points comprehensible to a sixth grader (i.e., an eleven-year-old!) It's necessary to make the points simpler and more basic in these cases because the brain receives and processes emotional arguments in the fight or flight region of the brain, the deeply-buried amygdala.

How can you determine the grade level of your answers? Microsoft Word has a grade level tool. To activate this feature in Word, click on the "tools" menu bar, select options, select the spelling and grammar tab, and select "show readability statistics." Thereafter, running "Spelling and Grammar" from the tools menu yields a report like this:

Readability Statistics	
Counts	
Words	820
Characters	3896
Paragraphs	24
Sentences	35
Averages	
Sentences per Paragraph	1.9
Words per Sentence	22.8
Characters per Word	4.6
Readability	
Passive Sentences	0%
Flesch Reading Ease	56.3
Flesch-Kincaid Grade Level	11.0

OK

How short? In his research, Dr. Covello discovered that we don't absorb long messages, so he came up with the 30, 10, 3 rule: The ideal soundbite is *no more than* 30 words. Spoken aloud, it takes *no more than* 10 seconds. And it is composed of no more than three sentences. (The preceding was 27 words long, could easily be spoken in under ten seconds, and was three sentences.) If you're asking yourself do *all* my answers have to be that short, my response is an emphatic, *no!* The key point, the *soundbite* part of your answer, should follow the rule. You can say a lot in 30 seconds. As an exercise, try reading from this book for 30 seconds and see how far down a page you get when the clock runs out.

The Rule of Three. If you think about it, unless you are the president of the Slow Talkers of the World, it's going to take you no more than eight or nine seconds to speak 30 words. Additionally, it would take a significant effort to craft a mere 30 into any more than three sentences. But I posed the rule in a set of three — 30 words, 10 seconds, 3 sentences. Why? Because for inexplicable reasons, the human mind wraps itself around a series of three and remembers them better than a single point (i.e.: 30 words) or any number of points above three. The rule of three will be useful later on when we are talking about countering negative arguments.

¶ **KOTJ: Knock off the jargon**. According to the *Guinness Book of World Records*, the world's longest acronym is: NIIOMTPLABOPARMBETZHELBETRABSBOMONIMONK-ONOTDTEKHSTROMONT. The Latin letters are an approximation, because they are transliterations from the original Cyrillic. In the old, bureaucratic Soviet Union, those fifty-six letters were shorthand for: "The Laboratory for Shuttering, Reinforcement, Concrete and Ferroconcrete Operations for Composite-Monolithic and Monolithic Constructions of the Department of the Technology of Building-Assembly Operations of the Scientific Research Institute of the Organization for Building Mechanization and Technical Aid of the Academy of Building and Architecture of the USSR." (And you thought the Soviet Union crumbled because it spent itself into insolvency keeping up with the U.S. in the arms race!)

If you dropped that acronym in an interview you would use an appreciable amount of the interview time just explaining it. As dense and incomprehensible as that old Soviet acronym is, the routine jargon you use daily may be just as incomprehensible to a reporter and to his audience. The fact is, every business, science, art, craft, and trade has its own jargon. What you and your colleagues instantly understand may leave outsiders in the dust. Sure those acronyms and the catchy lingo make your job easier, but they make the job of an interviewer and his end-user harder. Reporters have to translate your jargon and to avoid that chore, they may paraphrase you.

Sometimes we encounter dueling jargons — a phrase or acronym that means one thing to you and your colleagues and something completely different to people in another industry. Here's an illustration: I was doing media training at NASA's Jet Propulsion Laboratory, working with the engineers involved in landing the Curiosity rover on the surface of Mars. The engineers referred to "EDL." In television production, EDL is an acronym for edit decision list — the time code list generated by an editing system. After the second reference, I stopped one of the engineers and asked, "Why do you need an edit decision list to land on Mars?" He was confused, so I said, "EDL — edit decision list." He laughed and said, "EDL is our acronym for entry, descent, and landing." EDL: dueling jargons.

A reporter may stop you when you deploy jargon and ask you to define the terms. But that interrupts the flow of thought and steals time better spent deploying your agenda points. So make it a rule to avoid jargon. (A handful of acronyms have become universally understood and don't need explaining. People may wonder what entity you're talking about if you said "The National Aeronautics and Space Agency," but they will instantly know "NASA." Similarly, FBI and CIA are familiar to all Americans, as is FEMA, in the aftermath of Hurricanes Katrina and Sandy.)

Most jargon mystifies and nearly all acronyms are indecipherable to the public. If you find yourself uttering an acronym, define it after first usage: "HUD — or the Department of Housing and Urban Development — has teams...."

FIVE MORE QUOTEWORTHINESS TIPS

Brand
"Yes" and "No" Are Not Answers
Use Grabbers
Be Specific and Enumerate
Avoid Weak Words

¶ **Brand!** How many times have you turned on your radio or TV mid-interview and heard an author refer repeatedly to "my book" or "the book?" If he captured your interest, you're going to have a tough time at Barnes & Noble getting even the most helpful clerk to find "The Book" or "My Book." Music artists I train frequently talk about "My CD" or "My Album." When they do that I tell them I'm going to bring out a CD of my own called "My CD" and another called "My Album" because they've been helping me promote them. Similarly, how many times have you heard an interview subject say, "we" instead of giving the name of his company or organization? "We" is not a name. Try, instead, "We at Consolidated Ynot Corporation feel…" Branding is simple: if it's got a name, use it.

Think about the photographs of competitive skiers you see in the sports pages of your daily newspaper. Invariably, the skier holds her skis upright, alongside her head, logo side facing the camera. The skier in the photo is "branding" — planting the name of her ski company sponsor in your head and inferring that if you use her brand you'll ski as well as she does. There can be too much branding. Look at NASCAR race cars. If there were any more company logos posted on those vehicles they would need no paint. There are, in fact, so many logos that most of us don't pay attention to any of them. NASCAR drivers, too, are logo'd to the max. There is enough reading material on their uniforms to distract you from what they're saying.

The mandate to "brand" is a little less important when you're dealing with the print media — where there's that reread factor and a reader can hunt earlier in the story to find out what company or organization you're affiliated with. But why make them do the work? If you brand, the reader won't have to hunt. Besides, getting into good habits in one medium pays dividends in all media.

¶ **"Yes" and "no" are not answers.** "Yes" and "no" are the beginning of answers; the door-openers to your real answer. We don't merely want to answer questions, we want to use them to get to our agendas. In a trial, an attorney will ask for a yes or no response, but an interview is not a trial. Reporters don't want yeses and nos, unless they are the first word in a longer answer. In an interview, there is no such thing as a yes or no question, even if a reporter poses one that way. How many times have you seen an uncoached, unsophisticated individual who responds "yes" and "no" to most questions? In those instances the reporter often fills in the blanks left by the interviewee — always a less than satisfactory solution. I can recall one such interview on "Good Morning America" when Joan Lunden was interviewing a woman who answered yes or no — and only yes or no — to every question. So before moving on to her next question, Joan had to fill in the blanks. The interview went something like this:

> **Joan: "And so then you went to the hospital and you told them that your baby had a very high fever. And they admitted her?"**
> **Guest: "Yes."**
> **Joan: "Then they told you it was pneumonia?"**
> **Guest: "Yes."**
> **Joan: "But you didn't believe that?"**
> **Guest: "No."**
> **Joan: "You thought your daughter might have an allergy to something she'd eaten?"**
> **Guest: "Yes."**

Did Joan have to work extra hard? Yes. Was this a satisfying interview for the viewers? No. Did we ever invite that woman back on the show? No.

¶ **Use Grabbers.** A grabber is a word device or phrase that makes your message come alive. A grabber turns a *could use that* response into a *gotta use that* answer. A grabber can be a metaphor, simile, or word picture. It can be a comparison, or it can be a quote or the paraphrase of a quote. A grabber can be an attention-getting fact, like a remarkable statistic. Or it can be an "st" word — words that *end* in the letters "st" ("first," "last," "biggest," "smallest," "brightest," "fastest," etc.). The media love "st" words. Here are some examples of grabbers:

Word Pictures: "It's good to be open-minded, but no so open-minded that your brains fall out." -- Richard Sloan, professor of medical ethics at Columbia university discussing faith vs. medication in the treatment of diseases. Or, here is French satirist Stephane Guillon speaking about gaffe-prone Nicholas Sarkozy, the republic's former president: "Sarko is a treasure chest of blunders."

Comparisons: "A Nobel scientist is more likely to figure out Washington than a career politician is to figure out how to deal with carbon sequestration." Nobel laureate scientist Steven

Chu after the U.S. Chamber of Commerce derided his appointment as President Obama's first Secretary of Energy because, the Chamber said, he did not have the right skill set to survive Washington's cutthroat political environment.

Similes: "When the spokesperson got flustered at the news conference the reporters responded like sharks in a feeding frenzy."

Metaphors: "This proposal is the *Titanic* of economic planning — big, ambitious and doomed to sink."

Make sure your similes and metaphors work for and not against you. Possibly the most-quoted simile of the 2012 election campaign came from Mitt Romney's top political advisor, Eric Fehrnstrom explaining how the candidate — having campaigned in the hotly-contested primaries by saying he had been a "severely conservative governor" — was going to pivot toward the center in the general election: "Everything changes," Fehrnstrom told CNN, "It's almost like an Etch-a-Sketch. You can kind of shake it up and start all over again." (Incidentally, the candidate didn't do himself any favors using "severely." The dictionary definition of severe is "harsh; unnecessarily extreme." Another definition is "rigidly restrained in style." Sometimes the simple word "very" suffices nicely.)

A Quote or paraphrase of a quote: "Preparing for an interview, borrow this thought from John F. Kennedy and ask not what you can do for the reporter's agenda; ask what the reporter can do for your agenda."

Amazing fact or statistic: "In architecture, the Romans got it right. Every stadium and arena in the world uses the very same entrance and exit designs introduced in the Coliseum, back in 80 AD!"

"St" words: "NASA's New Horizons mission to Pluto is the *first* mission to the *last* planet."

Brief anecdote: "I am so convinced the ground water near our plant is safe that I just drank a glass of it and so did my three-year-old daughter."

¶ **Be specific and enumerate.** Specifics buttress your Positive Message Statements. The audience can infer the general rule from the specific case, but cannot infer the specific from the general rule. Specifics make a generalization come to life. What does "a lot of money" mean? It means two very different amounts to Warren Buffett and to me. Spell out how much money and the end-user can make up her own mind if it is a lot or not.

Also, enumerate. If there are three reasons why your company's plan is beneficial to the community, say, "There are three reasons for this..." and then tick off the three reasons. By citing the number in advance and then listing the points, you not only prepare the listener for them, but also you remind yourself to get to all three. It's best to keep the number of points to three if you can — remember the Rule of Three; that's the best number for comprehension.

¶ **Avoid weak words like "try" and "hope."** Try, hope, and hopefully are extremely weak words and usually unnecessary. "We plan to do..." is a lot stronger than, "We hope to do...." Similarly, "We're trying to get out of this situation," is a lot less confidence-building than the far more assertive, "We're going to get out of this situation." As I like to tell clients, "Try never to use the word, hope. Hopefully, you'll try hard enough to succeed." Two really weak sentences.

A LITTLE HOMEWORK FOR YOU

Using the grabber worksheet in the appendix, or one you create in your computer, develop grabbers for every one of your PMSs. You'll want to take your time with this exercise; for most of us grabbers don't just spring to mind. The simplest grabbers are comparisons, word pictures, or similes, so try for those first. The best way to craft a grabber is to ask yourself, "What everyday activity or concern can I equate with my message?" Thus, you might come up with, "Having a corporation change its orientation from being a growth stock company to becoming a value stock company is about as hard as making a U-turn in a subway train."

After you've written your grabbers, read them out loud to make sure they sound natural and that you're comfortable saying them. If you find them awkward, you'll want to massage them until they don't sound quite so foreign to you. Keep this worksheet handy on our desk or, if you created it on your computer, on your machine's desktop so they're readily available for you to refine them further over time. And always remember to jot down new grabbers as they occur to you. It's distressing to think about how many great grabbers have been lost forever because their authors felt they could remember them the next time they did an interview and didn't bother to commit them to paper or to a hard drive. It takes a great deal of preparation to appear spontaneous in an interview, but the result is worth the investment. Once you're ready with your PMSs and their supporting grabbers, you need to heed the next performance commandment:

COMMANDMENT 4:
THOU SHALT PRACTICE, PRACTICE, PRACTICE

I call this one the Henny Youngman commandment, as an homage to the late Henny Youngman, a comedian whose stock in trade was bad jokes. One of those bad jokes was: "Fella comes up to me on the street and says, 'Hey, how do I get to Carnegie Hall?' I says, 'Practice, practice, practice.'" Bad joke; good advice.

Here's an object lesson in practice, practice, practice from another old-time comedian, Milton Berle — the man who virtually invented television comedy. In the early days of "Good Morning America," we booked Berle as a guest on the show. I was thrilled because I had been a fan from a very early age. In fact, I think my parents bought our first television set so I would stay home on Tuesday nights and not slink off to friends' homes to watch "Uncle Miltie." I stopped by the dressing room where Berle was waiting so I could thank him for all those years of laughter. The door was open and when I stuck my head in, I saw Berle pacing back and forth, an unlit cigar in his hand, muttering. I stepped into the room, introduced myself as the show's executive producer and asked if everything was okay.

He said, "Yeah, sure, kid." (I was in my forties at the time.) "I was just rehearsing my ad-libs." Milton Berle was a veteran who'd done enough shows to earn the nickname "Mr. Television." If he had to practice, practice, practice before a five-minute interview, the rest of us have to practice, practice, practice, too.

If you are wondering how to practice for an interview when you don't know what you'll be asked, the answer is that with a little effort you can usually figure out the questions an interviewer will pose. If you did the homework in the last chapter you should have a pretty solid idea of the attitude, level of sophistication, and point of view of your interviewer and his outlet.

Write out the questions you think he will ask so you can practice deploying your agenda in response to them. Don't write questions like, "Gosh, you are a great fellow coming from a great organization. What can you tell me about yourself and about your organization that makes you and it so admirable?" Some interviewers might ask puffballs, but you'd better count on getting somewhat more challenging questions. Even the most benign reporter can ask them. In fact, here's our law about that:

THE EXPERIENCE MEDIA
FIRST LAW OF INTERVIEWS

**Anyone unprepared for tough questions
will be asked tough questions.**

Here's a case history: a financial services company was preparing a California test rollout of a new credit card product. They were going to hold a news conference and I asked them what tough questions reporters might ask so they could prepare responses. The lead spokesperson said, "Oh, we won't get any tough questions. This product is so great."

"O.K.," I said. "Pretend Ralph Nader is coming to the news conference. What will he ask?"

"Well," said the lead spokesperson, "he'd probably ask where he could sign up." That brought laughter from his fellow panelists. I again urged them to think of the tough questions and they kept insisting there were none.

I hardly need tell you what happened the next day when they held the news conference. The first question from the first reporter was worthy of a criminal prosecutor in its tone, severity, and insight. The panel just sat at their table with their mouths open. What followed was the journalistic equivalent of a shark feeding frenzy.

Interestingly, a year after the California introduction of the credit card product, there was a national rollout at a New York news conference and this time the spokespersons drilled extensively, developing persuasive answers to tough questions. They were ready for combat; no reportorial onslaught was going to take them by surprise. Curiously enough, nothing happened at the New York news conference. The New York and national reporters didn't ask a single tough question. But it's better to prepare for the tough questions and *not* get them than to be unprepared and suffer a barrage of them.

In the next chapter we'll compile a worksheet of tough questions and I'll teach you how to get from a challenging question to one of your agenda points. You'll need that information before you begin to practice, practice, practice. For now though, let me give you some techniques for practicing.

First of all, practice out loud. The down side of practicing by silently reading is you won't find the tongue-trippers until you're speaking them to a reporter — when it's too late.

To get used to hearing your message points in response to questions, have someone quiz you. Ask a colleague, friend, or family member pop questions at you. It's a lot more effective than asking yourself questions. Hearing the questioning words coming from an external voice, rather than from an internal one, will make them very real to you. Actors always "run lines" with another person — even if it isn't the individual with whom they'll play the scene. Running lines helps put those incoming words in a human context. In the same way, hearing questions asked by someone else — even an excessively friendly someone else — is more useful than imaging the questions from a phantom reporter.

There is no substitute for seeing yourself in action on video, even if you're prepping for a magazine or newspaper interview, so record all practice Q&A sessions on video. If you don't have a camera, use your smartphone. Then watch the video and grade yourself. Have your agenda point and grabber worksheets at hand so you can see how many of them you worked into the interview. It is important that you identify questions you could have used to get to a PMS but failed to use. Seeing the missed messaging opportunities in practice interviews will insure you don't miss them in real interviews. Keep practicing until you can work in all your PMSs and grabbers. That's *how* to practice. But before you begin those dry runs, you'll need to learn the fifth commandment.

COMMANDMENT 5:
THOU SHALT NOT LIE, EVADE, SPECULATE, NOR COP AN ATTITUDE

Aside from the moral and ethical imperatives against lying, there are very practical reasons — as evidenced by this sequence of quotes from Tour de France champion Lance Armstrong:

"I can emphatically say I am not on drugs." —1999
"We are completely innocent." — 2000

"I do not take performance-enhancing drugs." — 2004
"We're sick of these allegations….They're absolutely untrue." — 2004
"I have never doped." — 2005
"How many times do I have to say it? I've never taken drugs." — 2005
"As long as I live, I will deny it." — 2010
"If you're trying to hide something, you wouldn't keep getting away with it for 10 years. Nobody is that clever." — 2011
"I have never doped." —2012
"All the fault and all the blame here falls on me. I viewed this situation as one big lie that I repeated a lot of times…. I am sitting here today to acknowledge that and to say I'm sorry for that." — 2013

Here are two more examples:

"I did not have sexual relations with that woman."
- **President Bill Clinton**

A nine-word soundbite with ramifications that rendered a presidency ineffective for months on end.

"Read my lips, no new taxes."
- **George H. W. Bush**

A six word soundbite that may well have cost the first President Bush a second term.

By way of explanation, let's refer to a soundbite that pre-dates sound recording:

"It is true that you may fool all the people some of the time; you can even fool some of the people all of the time; but you cannot fool all of the people all of the time."
- **Abraham Lincoln**

Not all lies and other shadings of fact will be found out; but recent history shows just how damaging lies can be when the bright light of truth shines on them. In a strict, dictionary sense, Clinton was not lying, but rather he was evading — fooling the people — since Webster's definition of "sexual relations" is the act of coitus and, according to the participants, his illicit affair did not involve that specific act. You'll note the president did not say, "I did not have sex with that woman," but said, "I did not have sexual *relations* with that woman." Not a lie — by a verbal technicality — but certainly a lawyerly evasion.

In the same vein, how costly was it for Martha Stewart, when first accused of insider trading, to put out a story about previously instructing her broker to sell her ImClone stock when it dropped below $60 a share? How much more forgiving would the public have been had she said, "In the excitement of the moment, knowing what I knew, I made a mistake by acting on advance information. It was an unfortunate mistake and to make amends, I am donating the entire profit I made from that sale to the American Cancer Society." When Ms. Stewart finally did do an interview, she spoke with *The New Yorker* magazine legal correspondent Jeffrey Toobin — fully two months after the charges first surfaced — and declined to discuss the details of the case on the record. In the story that resulted from Toobin's interview, Ms. Stewart appears extremely concerned about the public's perception of her but does nothing to court public opinion, lacing her quotes with repeated egotistical comments. In other words, she copped an attitude — a pitfall we'll deal with in a moment. In fact, the Martha Stewart *New Yorker* interview is a virtual textbook example of how *not* to do a print interview. Chapter 8 treats this interview in more detail.

There is another practical reason for telling the truth in interviews and for that one I quote one of my mentors, the late Elmer W. Lower, former President of ABC News. He used to say, "Always tell the truth. That way you won't have to remember what you said." (Incidentally, that's a good grabber.)

In my earliest days at ABC, before becoming a producer, I was the director of public relations for the news division. One day Elmer told me that a major development concerning ABC News was coming, adding, "I'm not going to tell you anything about it so if you get a call from the press, you won't have to lie." The story was that ABC News had hired Harry Reasoner away from CBS. Not fifteen minutes after Elmer told me he wasn't going to give me details of the big story, I got a call from a Chicago newspaper columnist who had gotten wind of the story. He asked me, "What's all this about Harry Reasoner leaving CBS and becoming the anchor of the ABC Evening News?"

I could truthfully respond, "First I've heard of it."

What if telling the truth in an interview can land you in jail or subject you to a lawsuit? That would appear on the surface to be a good question, but if either of those scenarios are at all likely, why is your lawyer letting you talk to the media? The news media, unlike Congress, the state legislatures, and the courts, cannot compel you to appear and talk to them. Silence is a better response than falsehood.

Speaking of falsehoods and misrepresentations, don't deny saying something that TV cameras or radio microphones have recorded you saying. In 2006, presidential press secretary Tony Snow claimed that President Bush had used the term "stay the course" only seven times in connection with the Iraq war. That evening the fake news program "The Daily Show with Jon Stewart," displayed its journalism chops by showing video of Mr. Bush saying "stay the course" a total of 28 times. In addition to the "Daily Show" video becoming an instantaneous hit on YouTube, mainstream TV news shows began their own count, finding still more instances of the president using the term. More recently, in 2014, Mr. Bush's erstwhile political guru, Karl Rove questioned in a speech whether Hillary Clinton had sustained brain damage during a concussion incident. Then he went on Fox News and said he had not questioned whether Mrs. Clinton had sustained brain damage. His Fox colleagues did him the disservice of rolling a clip of him saying just that.

In the 2004 presidential campaign, former Vermont Gov. Howard Dean self-destructed with an on-camera scream to an assembly of his supporters. His campaign manager, Joe Trippi, told some reporters, "He wasn't thinking about the cameras." He should have been thinking about them — there were about a dozen trained right on him. If there are cameras and reporters in the room, it is naive to think they will exclude anything newsworthy they see or record. And, as both President Obama and Mitt Romney can testify, a good rule in today's media environment is that anybody with a smartphone should be treated like a reporter. Which these days means everybody almost everybody in every room.

THE DANGER OF SPECULATION

The reasons for not evading and for telling the truth in an interview are pretty obvious. But what can be the harm in speculating? In a news story all that separates a speculative comment from an assertion is one word: "speculated." The reporter writes, "he speculated," and it's clear that what she's quoting is your best guess. But what if the copy editor strikes the work "speculated" and substitutes, "said"? Your speculation has become an assertion. Even if the quote goes into one publication clearly identified as speculation, a second reporter, picking up the quote for a subsequent story, may omit the speculative tone. The first time you're quoted, it's speculation.   The next time, it's fact.

Here's an object lesson on speculation: a government agency was going to use a radioisotope power source on a project. Radioisotope power is frightening to some people, and in this instance the isotope was Plutonium, which is more daunting to many people than even Uranium. In an interview, one of the project engineers said, "This time around we have to use Plutonium. But by the time we build the next project like this, solar technology will have advanced so much we'll be able to use that." That quote appeared in newspapers. Well, solar wasn't sufficiently advanced when it came time to build the next project and opponents of radioisotopes sued to block the project, citing — among other things — the engineer's speculative quotation. The case was thrown out, the project was built using Plutonium and it was a great success. Nonetheless, the speculation in the media was a needless hurdle for the project.

If you speculate about something and subsequent developments prove you wrong, you may undermine your credibility. Whether it has its roots in speculation or oversight, error has an enduring shelf life; like the villain in a horror movie, it just won't die. Who can forget the photograph of American and Vietnamese employees clambering up the ladder toward a helicopter atop the roof of the U.S. embassy in Saigon when that city fell to the Vietcong and North Vietnamese? You likely know the photo: the ladder bows under the weight of the ten or twelve people on it, a man stands alongside the helicopter, reaching for the person at the top of the ladder; an iconic representation of the fall of Saigon. Except it isn't a picture of the U.S. embassy. Photographer Hubert van Es snapped a photo of CIA employees clambering toward a helicopter atop an apartment house near the embassy. Someone at UPI in Australia distributed it with an erroneous caption and for decades thereafter everyone thought it depicted the evacuation of the U.S. embassy. (Google still perpetuates the error; enter "Saigon Embassy, evacuation" in Google images to see the photo.)

The photo caption misidentification is a minor error, but its persistence shows you how hard it is to get the error genie back in the bottle.

COPPING AN ATTITUDE

The last part of the fifth commandment is Thou Shalt Not Cop an Attitude.*

This ought to be self-evident: Unless you are role-playing in your interview (young rebel actor, gangsta rapper, or a professional wrestler), you do yourself a disservice by copping a hostile, challenging, superior, or arrogant attitude.

Vice President Al Gore's supercilious demeanor in his first 2000 presidential debate against then-Gov. George W. Bush cost him dearly in the election. In the lessons unlearned department, Senator John Kerry adopted much the same superior attitude in the first of his 2004 debates against President Bush, with similar results. Martha Stewart's superior *noblesse oblige* attitude contributed to the media frenzy attendant upon her insider trading accusation. In December, 2005, then-Defense Secretary Donald Rumsfeld won himself few friends in this exchange in a town hall meeting with troops in Kuwait who were awaiting deployment to Iraq:

> **Soldier: Our soldiers have been fighting in Iraq for coming up on three years. A lot of us are getting ready to move north relatively soon. Our vehicles are not armored. We're digging pieces of rusted scrap metal and compromised ballistic glass that's already been shot up, dropped, busted, picking the best out of this scrap to put on our vehicles to take into combat. We do not have proper armament (sic.) vehicles to carry with us north.**
>
> **Rumsfeld: "I talked to the general coming out here about the pace at which the vehicles are being armored. They have been brought from all over the world, wherever they're not needed, to a place here where they are needed. I'm told that they are being - the Army is - I think it's something like four hundred a month are being done. And it's essentially a matter of physics. It isn't a matter of money. It isn't a matter on the part of the Army of desire. It's a matter of production and capability of doing it. *As you know, you go to war with the Army you have. They're not the Army you might want or wish to have at a later time.*"**

---

* Copping an attitude is an American idiomatic expression that may not be understood universally. For our purposes, copping an attitude means puffing yourself up, acting superior or impatient with your interviewer because you don't like his attitude or are dismissive of his level of sophistication in your field.

Interestingly, Rumsfeld had already answered the question before he copped his attitude, making it appear that his slighting of the soldier's concern was a gratuitous afterthought. In addition to that first seemingly callous statement, later on he added yet another comment that the troops in the room could easily have construed as dismissive: "And if you think about it, you can have all the armor in the world on a tank and a tank can be blown up. And you can have an up-armored Humvee and it can be blown up."

What part of Rumsfeld's answer ran on every newscast in America, was quoted in every newspaper in the world, and was featured on all radio newscasts? The part where he appeared to be patronizing the soldiers he was sending into harm's way: "*As you know, you go to war with the Army you have. They're not the Army you might want or wish to have at a later time.*" If you put a chip on your shoulder, the media will be more than happy to knock it off.

Now that we've gone over the five commandments of interviews and some interpretive analysis, let's move on to practical applications in interview settings. Let's first examine what you can expect to encounter and how you can turn the challenge of an interview into an opportunity to get your message out to a large and interested audience.

SUCCESSFUL
INTERVIEWS TOOLS

In Chapters 2 and 3 you learned how to prepare an agenda for an interview and how to tailor your messages for the media. Now let's look at interviews in greater detail. You'll want to master a specific set of skills — and understand the tricks of the reporter's trade — before you sit down for an interview. Not all your media encounters will be similar in tone and attitude, so at the risk of being annoyingly repetitious, let me reiterate: Before facing a reporter or taking her interview phone call, examine her media outlet and, if possible, her individual work to get some clues about how she will use your material and how she will treat you and your agenda points. In addition to the tone of the publication or broadcast and the work of the reporter, there are a few additional clues to a reporter's agenda and you'll want to investigate those.

You are always a leg up if she's working on a story that you or your organization initiated. In those cases — an announcement of a new product or service or unveiling an important discovery — reporters are responding to your agenda, so it is easier to keep the interviews on track. But when you are responding to someone else's announcement or to an interviewer's enterprise story — that is, one she initiated herself — the interview agenda is initially in the reporter's hands. That requires you to work harder in the interview to bring the questioning around to your messages.

The overwhelming majority of interviews are neutral or even friendly — not hostile and adversarial. But be aware that a friendly tone can mask a tough question. Not every inquisitorial reporter comes on with the pit bull determination and toughness of a Steve Kroft on "60 Minutes."   In fact, some of the most effective investigative reporters *don't* figuratively grip you by the neck and squeeze; rather, they cordially invite you to hang yourself.

One of the best investigative television correspondents I worked with was David Schoumacher who was very effective at getting people to stick their heads in his noose by asking the toughest questions in the friendliest way. He had a warm and charming smile and his tone was never challenging nor prosecutorial. As a result, he was able to get an amazing array of skilled corporate executives and politicians to make incriminating statements in the most matter-of-fact way. Because they were not on the defensive, their protective radar was off and they regularly gave up more information than they ever intended. The lesson here is to listen to the *words* of the question, not the *tone* of the question.

Early in the 20th Century, Ida M. Tarbell, the mother of investigative journalism, worked for years to research her book, *The History of the Standard Oil Company.* It was her masterwork, revealing illegal practices used by John D. Rockefeller to monopolize the oil industry in the United States. At the time, many men felt women could not grasp complex business concepts and so a lot of executives opened up to the "little lady," never expecting that her steel trap mind was not just grasping but was analyzing and understanding every nuance of what they were saying.

Why rehash this bit of ancient history? To emphasize that the way a reporter looks or acts is not a clue to her goal. Remember this: Even the most benign reporter sometimes comes up with tough questions.

You want to know how your interview fits into the larger picture the reporter is painting. So you or your public relations aides should ask these questions.

FIVE QUESTIONS FOR EVERY REPORTER

1. What is your story about?
2. Who else are you interviewing?
3. How much time will you need?
4. How long will your story be?
5. Do you need documents, props, photos, videos?

It's important you get the answers to these questions before you sit down with the reporter. You can pose them when she calls to arrange the interview or, as a last resort, ask them during the preinterview warmup. Reporters are often asked these questions and should be willing to answer them. This need not be a long, drawn-out discussion; a reporter can answer most of the questions with just a few words. Sometimes she'll tell you she doesn't know an answer. That may be truthful, because the story is a work in progress, or it may be an obfuscation. If you don't get straight answers to three or more questions, chances are the reporter is misleading you about the nature and direction of the story and you need to be on guard.

¶ **What is your story about?**   Ask this in a helpful way; you want to appear cooperative and outgoing. When you get a straightforward answer to this question you can, indeed, be much more helpful to the journalist. Try asking it like this: "I'd like to know the specifics of what your story is about so I can gather and review the appropriate materials and make sure I've got all the facts and figures you're going to need from me." Most reporters want you to be prepared; if you do the research in advance, they don't have to do it after the fact. Often if an interview does go beyond what the reporter indicated in advance, it will be because it naturally flows there. There are, however, a number of reporters and producers — usually working on the investigative publications and broadcasts — who will not give you a straight answer to this question. Ostensibly that's because they want the interview to be more spontaneous. Actually they want to give you as few clues to their agenda as possible so they can catch you unawares and trap you.

¶ **Who else are you interviewing?**   If he's interviewing four people from your company or organization, you should tailor your answers accordingly. ("Well, you're going to be talking to Sharon, and she is our authority on this issue. My own area of specialization is….") If he tells you he's also going to be interviewing competitors or opponents, you have the opportunity to second-guess what they've told him or will tell him and craft responses. Also, knowing his other interview subjects gives you the opportunity to suggest additional people to talk with — especially individuals who agree with your point of view. You might say to him, "That's a good list, but you might also want to talk to Dr. Hackley; he's the foremost independent authority in the country on…." Recommending other interview subjects who are independent of your company or organization enhances your credibility with reporters.

¶ **How much time will you need?** Knowing the answer to this question enables you to set limits on the length of the interview. If he says, "An hour," you can always say, "I'm afraid I can only spare twenty minutes." Then, if the interview is going well, stay longer. Be aware that some reporters habitually understate how much time they need because they hope that once you're sitting with them, you'll feel awkward about ending the interview. But if you've told the reporter in advance how much time he has, the control rests with you. "Well, Jim, I told you I could devote fifteen minutes to this interview and we've been here for fifteen minutes, so I'm afraid we've got to wrap it up now." Of course, if it's going swimmingly, you can say, "I know I told you I could only spare fifteen minutes for this interview, but I think I can squeeze in another five if you need it."

¶ **How Long Will Your Story Be?** Your answers can be a lot more expansive and detailed if the interview is for a *Rolling Stone* magazine piece that will run seven thousand words than if it is for a two-minute report on the local TV station's 11 p.m. newscast. You need this information to help you frame your answers appropriately. A truly skilled interview subject like director Stephen Spielberg, for example, gives a short form, quip of an answer to an interviewer who grabs him for a few seconds while walking down the Academy Awards red carpet on his way into the Oscar® ceremony. Asked virtually the same question on Bravo Network's leisurely and informative "Inside the Actors Studio" or PBS's "Charlie Rose," Spielberg will give a much longer, contemplative, and thought-provoking response. On the red carpet, he knows that his remarks will be one of dozens used in the Oscar® story, so he keeps it short; while the Bravo or PBS shows will focus exclusively or nearly exclusively on his thoughts and feelings, so he can be more expansive.

¶ **Do you need documents, props, photos, videos?** If you know in advance what support material will be helpful to the reporter, then you won't find yourself sitting opposite her saying, "I have a paper on that. I wish I'd brought it with me." Or, "You know, I've seen a really good photograph that illustrates that point. I don't know where it is, but if you could see it, I know you'd agree that it is terrific." Even if she says she needs nothing, you might want to bring to the interview props and video (for television), photographs (for all media) and releasable documents. Supply items that buttress your agenda's Positive Message Statements. As an example, not long ago I was doing media training for some astronomers who were talking about how different telescopes — infrared, x-ray, and ultraviolet — enhance our view of the universe because they can "see" what optical telescopes cannot. Their message really came home to me when I discovered on a NASA website identical pictures of Saturn taken through optical and ultraviolet devices. The familiar ringed planet in the ultraviolet photo had brilliant auroras at its poles, planetary wonders that were invisible in the optical photograph. I encouraged the astronomers to bring these photos — or others like them — to future interviews to illustrate their point.

HOW TO MASTER ANY INTERVIEW

Interview mastery *is* media mastery. A simple set of skills will empower you to work your agenda into any interview.

ENABLING YOUR AGENDA, DISABLING THE REPORTER'S AGENDA

Your goal in an interview is to enable your agenda; to not just answer questions but to *use* questions. As I noted earlier, if the reporter's agenda meshes with yours, then it's relatively easy. If the reporter's agenda diverges from yours, you need to disable his agenda in order to enable yours.

In general, reporters are interested in what's new, unique, and unusual. The cliché is: dog bites man is not news; man bites dog is news. These days, however, there is a premium on bad and frightening news (the fear "f" word journalism so loves), so dog bites man may once again be news — if the bite is severe enough or if enough dogs are biting enough men so the media can frighten people with a "trend." Conflict and drama also pique a reporter's interest. And good news such as so-called "miracle" cures, moneysaving schemes or tips, and safety information are all grist for the journalist's mill. Sometimes, then, your agenda will neatly match the reporter's needs — for instance when you are promoting a book on saving money by reducing energy consumption in your home or giving information about how to safeguard the health of audience members with a new medication or medical procedure. At other times, you may be on the defensive — when critics charge a product, policy or program you advocate is dangerous, costly, or ineffective.

In either case, take a piece of advice from the 19th Century Prussian general, Carl von Clausewitz who said "The best defense is a good offense." [Vince Lombardi said it, too, but von Clausewitz said it first.] If you heeded the Boy Scout Commandments in Chapter 2, then you know the agenda points you want to make, you are familiar with the tone and nature of the publication or broadcast, and you have identified your listener — the outlet's end-user, not the journalist. You also know that end-user's level of sophistication, and you're prepared to answer questions in a short and simple manner, lead with your conclusion, and brand your answers.

Getting your message across to the skeptical WSIC (Why Should I Care) listener is pretty easy when the reporter asks, "Tell me, my friend, have you any Positive Message Statements you'd like my readers [viewers, listeners] to know about?" But in the ten thousand-plus interviews I've overseen or conducted myself, I've never heard that question posed and I certainly never asked it. While reporters won't ask that question, they do come close with the commonplace interview-ending: "That about covers my questions. Is there anything you feel I've left out or that my readers [viewers, listeners] should know?" That question really is the equivalent of the "any Positive Message Statements" question I cited, and you should always take advantage of the opportunity and unlimber an agenda point in response. If you had five points at the outset of the interview and managed to work in only three or four of them, go to one of your unused messages. If you have already managed to work in all of them before the "anything else" question, revisit one of them. Revisit either your most important PMS or one you think you may not have articulated very well. You'll likely express it more effectively the second time, and the repetition will put your agenda point in verbal boldface for the reporter.

If a reporter asks the "anything else" question, it will be at the end of the interview, and there's no guarantee she will ask it. So you should pepper the whole session with your PMSs, and not wait for it.

BRIDGING: FOUR STEPS FROM A REPORTER'S QUESTION TO YOUR AGENDA

Obviously, a direct question that solicits one of your PMSs is the easiest way to work an agenda point into an interview. "So tell me about this new asthma medication your company has developed" is an explicit invitation to deliver an agenda point. Similarly, if the reporter praises you, your company, or your product, that's an open door through which you should push a PMS. For example, if the reporter says, "I'm hearing very good things from asthma patients about this new medication you've brought to market." Your response should not be, "Gee, thanks;" instead, say: "Yes and that's because…." and continue to a PMS.

If you finish answering a question and the reporter is searching his list of questions for his next query, you can fill the vacuum by saying, "Another thing that asthma sufferers will want to know is…." and go to another PMS. But a word of caution: fill pauses only in a *friendly* interview. A time-honored trick of a hostile interviewer is to pause after you've responded to a tough question, hoping you'll feel the pressure of the silence and go beyond the answer you intended to give.

If the reporter is not asking puffball questions, not throwing kudos your way, and not searching her notes for the next question, how do you work your messages into the interview? Well, you cannot do what Henry Kissinger did when he was secretary of state and began his press briefings by announcing, "Ladies and gentlemen, I hope you have your questions because I have my answers." The State Department press corps was a club and he could get away with that in the club. But most of us aren't in a club with reporters so we need to build a bridge to our agenda points using the following technique:

BUILDING A BRIDGE
TO YOUR AGENDA

1. Short Answer
2. Bridge
3. Agenda Point
4. Shut Up

The best way to explain this is to discuss each step of the process and then show you how it would be deployed in answer to a tough question. In the response, each step will be in boldface, so you can follow the process with ease.

1. Short Answer. You don't want to be — or even appear — evasive, so answer the question with a short response. Don't challenge the question by saying, "You should have asked me about Y instead of X and here's my answer to Y." That's the quickest way to turn an interview hostile. Incredibly, some people in public life actually do that. Lyndon Johnson was famous for it. "No, no, " he would say, "the question ought to be…." and he'd ask himself a question he wanted to answer. Unless you're President of the United States I suggest you steer clear of that. In fact, it's not a good idea even for the chief executive, since it will breed resentment in the press corps.

The short answer I'm talking about addresses the information sought, but not for long. For example, the question is this: "Why is your company still using the X7 aircraft when everyone feels it's obsolete?" You don't want to talk about the X7; you want to extol a new freight service. Well, here's how to use your answer to this off-the-point question to get to your agenda: "**At Ynot Freight Express, we are convinced the X7, which we've flown for fifteen years, remains viable.**" That responded to the question in short form. Notice the branding right at the top of the answer. It was "At Ynot Freight Express," and not, "We are convinced." The answer tells you who "we" are. As the spokesperson for Ynot Express, I want to talk about something new, so I need to bridge.

2. Bridge. The bridge you build need not be very elaborate; it is holding up nothing more weighty than a transition. The simpler and shorter the bridge, the better. Let's go back to the obsolete aircraft question. "At Ynot Freight Express we are convinced the X7, which we've flown for fifteen years, remains viable. **In fact we're so sure of its reliability**…." Not a terribly long bridge. Some bridges can be a single word: "but," "however," "and." Or the bridge can be a few words that enable a transition: "on the other hand," "in addition to that," "as a matter of fact."

3: Agenda Point. "At Ynot Freight Express we are convinced the X7, which we've flown for fifteen years, remains viable. In fact we're so sure of its reliability **that we are using that plane to launch our exciting new freight service which will save our customers a hundred million dollars a year without having a negative impact on our earnings**."

Step 4: Shut Up! If you stop talking after delivering your message, the chances are good the reporter will follow up with a question about that message. If you bring the answer full circle and refer to his original question, you're giving up control of the agenda and inviting him to reask his original question in different language. Place yourself in the mind of a reporter hearing this answer: "At Ynot Freight Express we are convinced the X7, which we've flown for fifteen years, remains viable. In fact we're so sure of its reliability that we're using that plane to launch our exciting new freight service which will save our customers a hundred million dollars a year without having a negative impact on our earnings. So of course we don't consider the X7 obsolete." What's your next question going to be about? The obsolete X7 or the exciting new freight service? The X7, because the answer brought your mind right back to the obsolescence issue. The interview subject didn't shut up. If the answer had ended with the point about the money saving to the customers and the impact on Ynot's bottom line, chances are greater the next question would be about the freight service.

Bridging to a PMS from a question is counterintuitive for many of us. In school our teachers always insisted we answer the question that was asked. Here, we're moving beyond the answer that we would have given in school to make a point we want to stress. In a scholastic setting — even in a social setting — this is bad manners. In an interview, it's your job. But here are a couple of caveats about bridging:

The longer it takes you to get to the your bridge, the less likely you are to cross it. Your answer — the first part of the four-step process — should be as brief as possible. Often an interview subject gets so wrapped up in giving a highly-detailed response to an off-point question he loses sight of the bridge and his agenda point. Remember, you want to *use* questions, not just answer them.

Avoid seque whiplash. If you are asked about the aircraft's safety, you can't bridge to the company's Christmas party. It is a bridge too far.

The easiest questions to bridge from are those you should not be answering in the first place. If you are asked a question outside your area of expertise or authority, your short answer is: "That's outside my area of expertise. I'll put you in touch with someone who knows about that." Your bridge is: "But what I can tell you is…."

FLAGGING:
INELEGANT BUT EFFECTIVE

Remember our first two soundbite radio stations: KPUF and KISS — Key Point Up Front and Keep it Short and Simple? Sometimes we start an answer fully intending to get our key point up front, but we neglect to do it. Or, we go on and on and on and get lost. This often happens when we are acknowledging a question in preparation for building a bridge. The acknowledgment takes so much time we forget to turn onto the bridge. What to do? I recommend a technique I call "flagging." Raise a flag and tell the reporter what's important. Typical flagging phrases are: "What's really important is…" "I can't emphasize strongly enough…" "What's vital for your readers to understand is…" Not as elegant as "but," "however," "on the other hand," but a flag is a form of bridging. A flag tells the reporter, "Everything I've said up to now is garbage, here comes the good stuff." She will hit her mental reset button and begin paying attention anew. Flagging is an inelegant solution, but it's effective. And it's certainly more useful than the most commonplace alternative: your voice trails off and you grimace, shrug and end with an inconclusive "….so?"

You can also flag sophisticated concepts: "This is a complex idea, but it's important…." "I'm going to cite some statistics, and they're really critical…."

THE EVIL EIGHT:
REPORTERS' DIRTY TRICKS

Can you use that bridge-building technique in a tough interview? You'd better; or you'll never work in your agenda. As a practical matter, many questions that sound probing or hostile are easier to bridge from than questions that are merely off-point. Here are the top eight reportorial dirty tricks and techniques to counter them.

Trick 1: Words in Your Mouth. We've all seen this one. An interview subject gives an answer and the reporter interprets it for him, putting words in his mouth: "So what you're saying is this decrepit airplane, as near to retirement as it is, is going to be the backbone of a new service you're offering your customers?" How do you respond? By taking back control of your words. "No, [short answer] what I'm saying is [bridge] we are so convinced of the reliability of the aircraft that we're building our exciting new freight using the X7; a service that is going to save our customers $100 million a year." (Notice we've declined the invitation to use the words "decrepit" and "retirement.")

Watch "60 Minutes" or one of the other investigative TV newsmagazine shows and you'll see this "so what you're saying" technique used frequently. It is much less common on shows such as "Today," "CBS This Morning," or "Good Morning America." A reporter usually follows "What you're saying is" by taking what you've said beyond your original meaning. But there is a more benign reason an interviewer puts words in your mouth. If she accurately is characterizing what you've said she may be doing it because she's hearing a *could use that* answer and is suggesting language that would make it a *gotta use that* answer. She's not only offering you another crack at your answer, she's coaching you to say it in language she's almost guaranteeing she'll use. In that instance your response should be to embrace her language, unless it does factual damage to your agenda point. I remember a medical interview where, despite the reporter's extensive efforts to get a physician to use the word "miracle," the doctor would not characterize a recovery that way. "So," the reporter said, "what you're saying is this isn't a miracle recovery?" "Exactly," the physician answered, then, "it is an exceptional recovery, an unusual recovery, and it may offer us clues about how to treat other patients with this condition. That's the way science advances — by analyzing what we know and researching what we don't. It's no accident that the last five letters of 'research' spell 'search.'"

Trick 2: The Big Lie. The premise of the question is false. Sometimes the reporter does this out of ignorance or shoddy research. And sometimes a reporter throws out a false premise to put her interview subject on the defensive. In either case, you must immediately correct the false premise. If the reporter believes the premise to be true and you don't correct it, it's likely to wind up in her story. If the reporter is doing it to trip you up, your immediate correction tells her you are wise to her game. For example: "We know that the X7 aircraft is so obsolete you are the only freight line in the country to use it." Your correction is all the acknowledgment you need before building your bridge: "No, that's not the case. Several other airlines that use the X7. [short form answer avoiding the negative word "obsolete"]. And, in fact [bridge] we are creating our exciting new flying freight service using the X7...."

Trick 3: Assault with a Deadly Question. The late "60 Minutes" correspondent Mike Wallace was the master of this one and his mantle has been assumed by numerous national and local TV reporters, too. (There is very little in it for a print reporter to act the tough guy — no one sees him doing it.) The reporter hurls a question at you: hard-charging, accusatory, inflammatory, and filled with hot-button words: "Do you expect that the American people will believe that an ancient aircraft like this is still viable and safe?" Reporters use deadly questions more to provoke emotion than to elicit fact. In response, remain unemotional; if you do and the interviewer prods you, he's in danger of looking like a bully. Calmly refute the charge, build a bridge and move on to your PMS: "Why, yes, I expect that the American people to believe X7 is reliable [short form answer] and [bridge] so do we at Consolidated Ynot because we're using that aircraft as the basis for our exciting new...." Don't answer the tone of the question, answer the text of it. Stripped of its dramatic delivery, the question really was, "Is the X7 still viable and safe?"

Let me give you a case history about the importance of remaining calm in the face of hostile questioning, one in which the target of my investigative report outfoxed me. The story I was producing for the ABC newsmagazine show, "The Reasoner Report," concerned contaminated meat in supermarkets. My correspondent and I confronted a Connecticut State Health Department food inspector with an accusation that he had taken bribes to look the other way when he found violations in a particular market. We had very specific charges against the man, but they came from a single witness and there was no hard evidence like photographs or documents to back up her assertion. Our only hope to nail the inspector was to get him to admit it or to deny it in a shifty, guilty way — or, better yet, to run away. There's nothing as dramatic in television news as someone running away from the camera with a correspondent in hot pursuit, shouting questions. In the case of the meat inspector, my correspondent threw the bribery charge at him in the form of an accusatory question delivered in the tone and style of a TV prosecuting attorney. At the very least, we expected him to begin sweating and shifting, stumbling and bumbling. But instead, of the great theater we were expecting, he calmly and simply said,

"No. That's not the case. Never happened. I would never do that." Needless to say we didn't use the interview or the charge against him. Had he been media trained, he might have gone on to add, "What I look for when protecting the public health is...."

Trick 4: The Dire Hypothetical. The reporter presents a disastrous scenario and invites you to comment on it: "What would happen if you discovered that the entire fleet of X7s had to be taken out of service immediately to have their engines and controls replaced?" Again, the short form answer is easy. First label the premise of the question: "That's a hypothetical proposition that has no basis in fact or historical record. [short form answer] A much more likely scenario [bridge] is that these planes will continue to serve our customers well as we announce our exciting new...." Your short form answer identified the nature of the question. Then you presented your own, more likely hypothetical scenario, and moved on to your PMS. Sometimes a reporter will invite you to come up with the nightmare hypothetical: "What's the worst thing that can happen?" If he's too indolent to invent his own disaster, don't do it for him. Instead, decline to speculate or present a mild scenario: "The worst thing that can happen is that we may be delayed a few weeks as we do all the engineering tests that guarantee the success of this exciting new...."

Trick 5: The Interruption. Rather than waiting for you to finish a statement, the reporter jumps in, stopping you cold, throwing another question at you. This happens mostly in antagonistic broadcast interviews where the reporter is role-playing. He's the crusading good guy and he's going to get to the bottom of this! The best way to turn this rude technique to your advantage is to highlight the fact that the reporter is deploying it. Answer, "Well, I was about to say ...." And move on to your PMS. Unspoken in your response — but clear to viewers and listeners — is the phrase, "before you so rudely interrupted me." If he persists, you may want to call attention directly to it, "You know, Peter, a number of times you've interrupted me before I finished my thought. What I'd like people to know is...." And insert a PMS right there. Calling attention to his rudeness will usually cure it. Few reporters want to appear to be boors. As with the assault with a deadly question it is unusual for print reporters to employ this trick; there is nothing in it for them, whereas a broadcast journalist gets to appear tough and uncompromising when he interrupts.

Trick 6: The Filibuster. Some reporters think they know so much or love the sound of their own voices so ardently they hog *your* interview. Often this is true when the reporter is a specialist, eager to show off his knowledge. His questions become miniature speeches followed by "Would you agree?" or "Don't you agree?" It may be tempting to sit quietly by while the reporter gives you a pass by asking very few questions, but you will miss the opportunity to insert your agenda points if you let him get away with it. What to do? Well, when he throws one of those "Would you agree" questions at you, say, "Yes." [short answer] As a matter of fact, [bridge]...." and launch into one of your PMSs. If you disagree, say, "No. [short form answer] In point of fact, [Bridge],..." and deliver a PMS. Now if he persists in these filibusters and doesn't even bother to ask you to agree or disagree with him, find an opening and jump in. Listen carefully and when he makes a point you agree with (or disagree with), express your agreement (or disagreement) and bridge to a PMS. It's better to interrupt him when he's made a point with which you agree so you won't appear to be *quite* so rude. You can also jump in when he pauses to draw a breath; even the most enthusiastic filibusterer must breathe.

Early in my television career I worked with a reporter who had a specialty beat and fancied himself more knowledgeable than most of the people he interviewed. He was, in fact, extremely well-versed and usually was far better able to express the complex ideas of his field than many of the people he interviewed. He really wanted to interview only himself, but the management at ABC News, where we worked, would not have permitted that. Since he couldn't interview himself, he instead made long pronouncements and then asked his interview subjects, "Don't you agree?" After a while some of them were reduced to just nodding assent. It made my life hell when I edited the story. The more media savvy of his victims would say, "Yes, I agree...." and then express the same point in their own words, giving me *something* to work with. But many others were struck mute by his egotistical interviewing style.

Trick 7: The Pregnant Pause. I told you to take advantage of a pause in a friendly interview. When a reporter searches his prepared questions for the next one to ask, I advised, jump in with a PMS. But don't do it in an unfriendly interview. Hostile reporters use pauses, too, but not to find their next question. They use them as an invitation for you to expand on answers you've already given — invitations to go where you really don't want to go. I first became aware of this practice when I accompanied Harry Reasoner, then anchor of ABC's network newscast, to a guest appearance on the "David Frost Show." Harry and I had been on a week-long promotional tour for ABC News and the Frost show in New York was our last stop. Having listened to Harry give interviews for a week, I had heard all of his quip-filled, clever answers to the predictable questions. But when Harry delivered one of these to Frost, the Briton nodded, looked at Reasoner, and said nothing. Whereupon Reasoner, feeling the weight of the silence, jumped in and added to his stock answer. Frost did this several times during the interview.

When we left the studio, Harry said, "That Frost is a master of the pregnant pause. He got more out of me than any of the others this week and he did it by keeping his mouth shut." So here's the rule: if your interviewer pauses because he is searching for his next question, jump in. If he pauses because he wants you to say more than you want to say, don't take advantage of his silence. Usually, it's easy to tell the difference: the question-seeking reporter looks at his notes, sometimes frantically; the pregnant pause reporter looks you in the eye.

Trick 8: The False Equivalency.

Sometimes, to drum up controversy where none actually exists, reporters grant false equivalency to a specious argument. We see it all the time on cable news shows. Ninety-seven percent of climate science reports agree that the global climate is warming and human activity is a major factor in that change. Yet, in order to appear fair or to gin up some drama, TV news stages "debates" between a well-credentialed climate scientist and an outlier denier or skeptic. Similarly, in an interview, a specious argument may be offered to you in the form of a question and you may be asked to respond. The most effective way of handling this is to label it. "What you are doing is creating a false equivalency. You have asked me to respond to a fallacious and specious argument that is not based on the facts.[Answer] In point of fact [Bridge] Insert agenda point and grabber. Another example of stretching to create a controversy is the media's penchant for granting equal weight to the vaccinations-cause-autism arguments of comedienne and Playboy centerfold Jenny Mc-Carthy versus physicians and public health authorities from organizations like the American Pediatric Association and the Centers for Disease Control. Even after the British study that purported to uncover the link was exposed as a total fraud and its author thoroughly discredited, media outlets continued to grant Ms. McCarthy abundant exposure in her campaign against vaccination. Ms. McCarthy, after gaining a berth on ABC-TV's The View in 2014 said she is not anti-vaccination, ignoring the fact that there are decades of video clips, audio soundbites as well as abundant print articles chronicling her crusade. Her tenure on The View was brief; less than a year.

Responding to these eight dirty tricks, it's important you remember the teachable moment from former Health and Human Services Secretary Kathleen Sebelius that I cited on Page 44: don't repeat negative phrases or words embedded in the reporter's questions.

Also, don't introduce negatives on your own. During the height of the Watergate scandal, President Nixon told a news conference, "I am not a crook." Well, no one had asked him if he was a crook; he just threw out the negative without any prompting from the White House press corps.

ELEVEN RULES FOR ACING AN INTERVIEW

There are eleven rules you need to follow in order to prepare for and ace a tough or hostile interview. It's a good idea to follow these rules for all interviews, because, as I wrote earlier, even a kindly reporter can turn tough.

Rule 1: Play Reporter. Using Worksheet 4 in the Appendix, write down the toughest questions a reporter might throw at you. If you don't list and study the questions that keep you up nights, you won't be prepared when a reporter springs them on you. Remember our Law of Interviews: anyone unprepared for tough questions will be asked tough questions. The unprepared are magnets for tough questions.

Rule 2: Answer the Tough Questions. It does you no good to anticipate those tough questions if you don't also prepare your answers. Look at each of those questions and decide which of your agenda points you might be able to bridge to. As an exercise, pair a PMS with each of your tough questions. You may find some tough questions just can't accommodate a bridge. For those questions, come up with short, non-evasive, unambiguous answers. (Emphasis on *short!*)   But be forewarned, if you don't bridge the next question is likely to be a follow-up on the tough subject, whereas if you do bridge there is a fighting chance that you've set the interview on a new track — one leading to your agenda.

Rule 3: Rehearse Tough Questions. Have someone ask you those tough questions and record the session on video. Tell your inquisitor to be merciless with you.   When you screen your video, grade yourself on how well you did in building bridges from the questions to your messages.   Even if you did well the first time, repeat the exercise.   You want to get almost comfortable under a barrage of withering questions. The key word here is "almost."   You want to be *almost* comfortable, but not *totally* comfortable. You never want to be so relaxed and overconfident in an interview that you forget that you are working.

Rule 4: Record the Interview. Your best defense against misquotes in print or having answer A paired with question B in a broadcast story is to record your interview on audio or video. Be sure to let the reporter know you are recording it; this will put her on notice that she'd better quote you accurately and in proper context. Immediately after the interview, listen to the recording to make sure you didn't misspeak.   If you find you did, call the reporter at once, tell her you gave her an incorrect fact or expressed yourself incorrectly and supply the accurate answer or information. (Be sure to record this conversation, too.   It will be your only evidence that you corrected your error). Thirteen states and the District of Columbia as well as the Commonwealth of Puerto Rico have laws requiring that you inform all parties to a conversation or phone call if they are being recorded; the other states and the federal government permit unannounced recording of conversations and phone calls.   But it is a good policy from both ethical and practical points of view to announce that you are recording the interview even if your state permits clandestine recording. Ethically, you're laying all your cards on the table. Practically, you're putting the reporter on notice that you'll have proof if she distorts your answers.

Rule 5: Bring a Witness. In addition to recording the interview, you should have a witness on hand. It helps to have a knowledgeable colleague from your department or your public relations staff sitting in on the interview. Occasionally, under the pressure of the moment, you might misspeak, give an incorrect fact or figure, or get a name wrong. Your less-pressured colleague can intervene and offer you the correct information. Obviously, this doesn't work in a live broadcast interview, but in other formats it can be helpful. The colleague should not interrupt your answer mid-sentence to correct you. She should wait until you've finished your reply at very least and, in the case of a broadcast interview, she should wait until the camera has stopped recording before speaking up, so that her correction doesn't became a part of the on-air story.

Rule 6: Remain Calm. On pages 77 and 78, I dealt with assault with a deadly question. Broadcast interviewers ask these in hopes they'll result in the drama of a flustered or angry response; in fact the emotion is more important to this reporter than the facts of the story. (More on that in Chapters 6 and 7). You can remain in control of the agenda only if you remain unemotional. By unemotional, I don't mean being a flatliner wearing a toe tag on a hospital gurney. I mean avoiding displays of anger or guilty nervousness. Even impatience is perceived as a negative emotion by television viewers. As I've already pointed out, this was something Vice President Al Gore learned in the first 2000 presidential debate with Texas Gov. George W. Bush. Gore conspicuously rolled his eyes as Bush responded to questions. Rather than highlight the Texas governor's lack of verbal elegance, which was Gore's likely intent, the Vice President's exaggerated exasperation made him appear arrogant.

While the challenge to exhibit the correct emotion is especially acute in television interviews, even print reporters can use your facial and verbal excesses if you display them. "His face flushed with anger and his voice rising, Mr. Goodhue snapped a defense of Ynot Corporation against...."

The better prepared you are with PMSs and grabbers, with answers to anticipated tough questions, and with bridges to your agenda, the easier it will be for you to remain calm and in control and the less "snapping" you'll do.

Rule 7: Don't Go Off the Record. Anything you say to a reporter can be used. She might paraphrase, but the facts can wind up in print or on the air. If you're tempted to go off the record, be aware that reporters, publications, or broadcasters may not protect your identity. You think you've said something off the record, but the reporter thinks it's for attribution and, once he acts on his understanding, it *is* on the record. Even a reporter who promises to keep something you've told him in confidence may succumb to pressure from his superiors to put it on the record. Today, in the aftermath of the trial of vice presidential aide Lewis "Scooter" Libby for lying and obstructing an FBI investigation, a lot of journalists and sources are rethinking the whole concept of off the record. The Libby case, involving the leak of a covert CIA agent's identity, left in its wake several tarnished reputations, destroyed careers, and many newly cautious reporters. Judith Miller, formerly of *The New York Times*, spent eight weeks in a jail cell after she refused a judge's order to reveal a news source. (The source turned out to be Libby.) A lot of reporters now realize they have been tools of off the record sources who were merely using them, and they may be less willing to accept off the record comments than they were in the past.

Rule 8: Don't Supply Not For Attribution Information. A variation of Rule 7 and a favorite trick of government and some private sector officials: give reporters information on a not-for-attribution basis as in: "A high-level official of the Ynot corporation, requesting anonymity, told the Daily Bugle that …." It's usually pretty easy to trace the source of the quote. So if you're giving a statement "not for attribution" in order to keep out of the whistleblower's spotlight, don't do it; it's likely you'll be found out. It doesn't take a very sophisticated reader to figure out who the speaker is in most stories. And in some situations, the speaker is a virtual given. For example, the "high-level State Department official traveling with the secretary of state" who gives all those frank assessments of foreign leaders *is* the secretary of state and has been for the last 50 years. Since this charade is no secret to the worlds of politics, diplomacy, and journalism, it is a mystery to me why all parties continue to play it; but the little game persists.

Rule 9: Never Answer, "No Comment." Saying, "no comment" in an interview is like taking the Fifth Amendment in a congressional hearing or in court. True you're within your constitutional right to avoid self-incrimination, but invoking the Fifth *looks* incriminating. The perception is that the Fifth Amendment invoker has something to hide. Similarly, "No comment," looks evasive, largely because it is evasive. As the late comedian George Carlin said, "No comment *is* a comment." If you can't answer a question for a valid reason, use that reason as a short answer and build a bridge to a PMS. Here's how to do it: First, without using the words "no comment," tell the reporter why you can't answer his question. It may be that the query seeks information involving active litigation, and company policy or a judge's admonition prevents you from speaking. It may be that the question is about a matter outside your area of expertise or authority. Or it may be that the answer would reveal proprietary information and put your company at a competitive disadvantage. By announcing why you can't address the question, you've actually given the short answer that sets you up to build the bridge to your PMS. Here's an example: "I can't answer that because it's a matter that's in active litigation and the judge has imposed a gag order [short form answer] But what I can tell you is...[bridge]" Then insert your message and illustrate it with a grabber. Finally, shut up! Don't go full circle and finish your answer, "And that's why I can't address your question." If there is no judicial admonition against discussing the case, you can say, "company policy prohibits talking about matters that are in litigation."

Looking back, notice I started the statement with "I can't answer" not "I can't comment." Another alternative is, "I really can't address that because...." And then bridge to what you *can* address. Remember we want to use an answer to get to an agenda point. "No comment" slams the door on using the question. You can't very well say, "No comment, but I will tell you....."

Rule 10: Don't Guess. Guessing at an answer is dangerous; you could be wrong. But if you don't know an answer, use that lack of knowledge as a short form response: "I don't know. I can find out. [short answer] But what I do know [bridge] is that .... [Insert PMS]" Don't be bullied into guessing. Following your initial answer a prosecutorial reporter might thunder, "You don't know? You don't know? How can you not know? Isn't it your job to know?" Don't let him shake you up so much that you begin guessing. Stay resolute: "That's right. I don't know, but I'll find out and get that for you. What I do know is...." and move on to a second PMS.

Rule 11: Don't Understand the Question; Don't Answer the Question. I was media training a group of European scientists involved in a research project. The common language was English, so the training was in English as were the practice interviews. I asked a French physicist this question: "If this is so safe, why do you have contingency plans?" He gave me a relatively long answer, then stopped himself, leaned forward and said, "I'm sorry, what is a contingency plan?" "Why did you answer the question if you didn't understand it?" I asked. "I wanted to be polite." His good manners could have led to a problematical response. If you don't understand a question, don't answer it, don't guess at its meaning. Ask for clarification or try to rephrase it yourself, "If I understand your question, you want to know....." This allows you to restate the question more to your liking. Obviously, this doesn't work with a very simple and direct question like, "How long will it take to clean up the toxic spill in your factory's backyard?" To justify rephrasing, a question has to have some nuance — even some ambiguity — to it. Also, your restatement has to have more than a passing similarity to the original question. For instance, you can't say this: "What you're asking me is how effective our affirmative action policy has been...." if the original question was: "Were you here when the chemical spill polluted the ground water?"

BUT WAIT, THERE'S MORE

Here are some additional tips for effective interviews:

¶ **Be Specific.** The media love specifics. Anytime you can give a case history or a concrete example of a general concept, you are communicating effectively.

A reader or listener can infer the general concept from the specific, but cannot infer the specific from the general concept. You can use specifics introducing or concluding general statements. It's not enough to say, for instance, "The space program has given society lots of technological and scientific advances." The reader of the newspaper or the viewer of a TV broadcast containing that quote is also listening to that universal radio station WSIC, Why Should I Care. If your quote ends there, he will mentally ask: "Oh yeah, like what?" Fill in that blank; answer that question before he asks it. Give him specifics that back up the generalized statement. For instance, "The space program has given society lots of technological and scientific advances. Walk into the radiology department of any modern hospital and you will see diagnostic tools such as MRIs that were developed as an outgrowth of technology created for the space program." The specific brings home the Positive Message Statement.

¶ **Cool down post interview.** I have concluded interviews and seen the subject leap up out of his seat and begin sprinting from the room, only to be halted by the microphone cable attached to his tie. Resist the urge to flee; the post interview cool down can be as important as the preinterview warmup.

In the cool down, as in the warmup, don't say anything to the reporter you don't want the whole world to hear, but use the time to plant additional ideas. For example, don't say, "Gee, I'm so glad you didn't ask me about XYZ; I was really afraid of that one." That injunction may sound like a given to you, but a number of interview subjects have expressed just that sentiment to me over the years using a variety of stunningly naïve phrases like that. My instinct on hearing that was to dive right in, probe deeper. I've stopped crews packing their gear and had them reset their lights, and begin shooting after hearing a comment like that.

Use the cool down to suggest additional resources to the reporter — resources that back up your point of view. "You know, if you're interested in learning more about this, I'd suggest speaking to Dr. Harley. He's done a lot of research in the field." Or, if you realize that you've failed to get one of your key messages into the interview, bring it up during the cool down. The reporter may not go for the bait, but you've nothing to lose by dangling it. In a print interview, a reporter can seamlessly integrate that additional message into his story and the reader won't know it was an afterthought. In a broadcast story, the reporter might use the information by saying on-camera, "Mr. XYZ also told me that Ynot Corporation is contemplating doubling its dividend next quarter."

THE GOOD INTERVIEW AND the GOOD GUEST

In my newspaper years, there were a number of people I would go back to time after time for comments on stories. They were the print equivalent of television's good guests. A good guest or good interview is someone who makes the reporter's job easier by preparing, speaking clearly and comprehensibly, and giving good, pithy, even entertaining, quotes.

Most good guests are thought-provoking. They may accomplish this through deft use of language, introduction of new and fresh information, or insightful viewpoints on information in general circulation. Or they may get our attention by throwing the biggest verbal bricks through the biggest plate glass windows. You can be a good guest if you are well prepared, use precise language, easily grasped specific examples or case histories, and sprinkle your interviews with trenchant grabbers. When I was executive producer of "Good Morning America," the prolific author Isaac Asimov lived directly across the street from our studio. Asimov wrote science fact and science fiction books — producing two to three books and dozens of magazine articles a year — so he always had fresh subjects for us. And, importantly, he was a good talker — articulate, comprehensible, accessible, entertaining. We hatched a deal with Asimov: any time a guest failed to show up for an appearance on "Good Morning America," we would phone him and he would walk across the street and fill the absent guest's slot by talking about his latest book or article. It was a wonderful arrangement; he always had something interesting to say and we always had emergency access to a guaranteed good guest. Now maybe your goal isn't to be some publication's or broadcast's equivalent of Isaac Asimov, but you will know you have succeeded if, at the end of an interview, the reporter tells you, "That was good. Do you mind if I or my colleagues call on you again in the future?"

DON'T "DO LUNCH"

For me, a meal is a meal and an interview is an interview; never mix the two. There are too many distractions at a mealtime interview. If the food is good, the reporter may spend valuable space praising it in his article. And if the food is bad, he may waste space complaining about it. You've read those stories: first the reporter describes the ambiance, then the diners, then the service and food, and then — almost as an afterthought — she writes about her interview subject and what he had to say. All that verbiage wasted on ambiance, crowd, and food when it could have been about you and your agenda!

Also, all restaurants are full of clatter and chatter, which distract from your primary reason for doing the interview. In the world of broadcasting, you may find yourself trying to talk with your mouth full — which is never attractive. In a print interview, the surroundings may so distract the reporter she misses some of your major points. Finally, if you spill a drink, choke on a forkful of steak, or accidentally drop your butter knife on your lap, the mishap could end up in the article, making you look clumsy, careless, or ill-mannered. Even if the reporter offers to pay for the meal — and *that* will be the day — don't do it. Similarly, an interview over cocktails is an invitation to disaster for obvious and subtle reasons. If the drink you have with a reporter is nonalcoholic or even if an alcoholic drink doesn't affect your performance, she can still write, with perfect accuracy, "Interviewed over drinks, Mr. Fields said....," giving the impression alcohol may have impaired your answers. And if an alcoholic beverage consumed during an interview *does* affect you, it would be exceedingly surprising in this era of tabloid journalism for a reporter not to mention it in her article: "Slurring his words, Mr. Baccus said...."

The tips in this chapter pertain to all interviews in all media. You need to master additional, unique skills to be most effective in broadcast encounters. It won't hurt to employ the broadcast skills in print interviews as well. Communicating with all media using the broadcast skill set will make you a livelier, more interesting, more quoted interviewee. And, you won't have to keep changing styles when going from print to broadcast and back. More on television's unique demands in the next chapter.

CATERING TO THE ONE-EYED BEAST: TELEVISION APPEARANCES

If you are going to appear on television, watch television. I don't mean "Modern Family" or "Survivor." I mean informational programming, news, interview shows, and especially shows on which you're likely to appear. Watching a program lets you know what to expect when it's your turn before its cameras. Is the show live or live-to-tape and unedited or lightly edited ("Charlie Rose," "Meet the Press," "Good Morning America") or taped and heavily edited ("60 Minutes," "Dateline NBC," "20/20")? Is the show serious ("The News Hour," "This Week") or flippant ("The Daily Show," "The Minority Report")? Are guests interviewed singly or are they pitted against each other? And, if they are pitted against each other, are they expected to have a reasoned conversation ("The News Hour") or engage in an angry shoutfest? (Chapter 7 will have notes on how to handle yourself in a shoutfest.) Does the host have a political or social agenda (John Stossel on Fox, Nancy Grace on CNN, Chris Matthews on MSNBC)? Or is he journalistic (Anderson Cooper on CNN, Margaret Warner on "The News Hour")? Does the host listen to answers or just read a list of prepared questions and never follow up? Is he polite or tough to the point of being hostile? Is he out for information or for a laugh? Are you seated or standing? Is everyone dressed casually or formally? Are interviews long or short? If it's an edited show, are the soundbites generally lengthy and substantive or brief and vapid?

Watch the show and you'll answer all those questions. You'll learn nature of the audience, too: who is watching and what are do they want to hear about? You'll speak differently to an audience of businesspeople on CNBC than you will to a general audience like the viewers of the three network early morning news programs. Your audience may be sophisticated and knowledgeable news junkies ("The News Hour") or it may be more frivolous ("The Ellen Degeneres Show," "The Talk"). The more familiar you are with the show, the talent, and the format, the more at ease you'll be and the better prepared to unleash your agenda points.

When Hillary Clinton began promoting her book "Hard Choices" in June, 2014, she gave the first in her series of "exclusive" interviews to Diane Sawyer. Sawyer is a couple of years older so Clinton knew the ABC News anchor could not credibly question whether the former Secretary of State was too old to seek the Presidential nomination. In fact, when Sawyer broached the subject, Clinton responded brightly, "Isn't it great to be our age?" (Coincidentally, a month later Sawyer announced she was stepping down from her ABC anchoring post.)

THE NATURE OF THE BEAST

Early in my television career I worked on an investigative news magazine program headed by a veteran executive producer who was fond of proclaiming, "Television is a visual medium." He then disproved that by "watching" the first cut of my stories with his eyes closed. He did that so he could get the full essence of the written script and spoken soundbites without the distraction of the visuals. Back in those days television news reports were filmed, not videotaped, and the picture and soundtracks were separate. Once, as a gag, I had the editor play a first cut of one of my pieces for the executive producer without running the picture. The report ran its full four or five minutes, the screen blank, the sound track at normal level. When the piece ended, the executive producer opened his eyes, said, "That was pretty good; let's see it again." On the second run, the editor ran the picture and the soundtrack.

Notwithstanding my juvenile act of mischievous insubordination, that old boss of mine was right: although it is a blend of words and pictures, television *is* much more heavily dependent on images than any other medium. In fact, some stories are almost exclusively picture-driven.

Some years ago, *Consumer Reports* gave an unsatisfactory rating to an imported SUV because the magazine's testing engineers got one of them to tip over in a high-speed, lane changing maneuver. It was an interesting story to hear on the radio or read in a newspaper, but it was a riveting story to see on television. That was because the magazine supplied networks and stations with tape showing the vehicle speeding into a curve and tipping violently, two wheels lifting off the blacktop. Only a device similar to bicycle training wheels that was affixed to the SUV kept it from actually going over on its side. The strong visual impact of this TV story made it impossible for the manufacturer to counter with mere words. Instead, the company had to stage and film its own test of the vehicle.

When you are preparing for a television interview, think about whether there are visuals — tape, stills, animation, props, even drawings — that will help you make your points. In the SUV case, the best media defense was not a corporate engineer telling TV cameras that the *Consumers Reports* test was biased, but was the video of a test commissioned by the manufacturer and conducted by an independent engineering laboratory.

Television loves visuals, so think visually. Viewers, unlike my old boss, will be watching as well as listening, so any images you can produce to buttress what you are saying will help immeasurably.

I made this point in a media training session with some engineers who were about to deploy a device that used a small amount of a radioisotope for heating scientific instruments in a hostile climate. They feared that antinuclear activists might mount a scare campaign against them and public reaction would threaten the project. When I told the engineers to think visually, one of them pulled a pencil from his pocket, twisted off the tiny pink eraser, tossed it out on the table in front of him and said, "This is how much plutonium we need for this device." It was a dramatic and graphic demonstration. The most fevered stretch of the imagination could not visualize a nuclear weapon's characteristic and fearsome mushroom cloud fueled by such a trivial amount of material. "Do that in every interview," I suggested. "Especially TV interviews. It should put the controversy in perspective instantly."

I like to tell clients to consider television news to be the equivalent of a seven-year-old boy. How do you win over a seven-year-old boy? With a toy. For television, toys are props and videos. Supply a prop and/or video to a TV news producer and you go a long way toward controlling the finished story.

That's why presidents enhance their major addresses with charts, graphs, photographs, and even backdrops with message keywords printed on them in a repeat pattern. That's why NASA spokespersons usually have model spacecraft on their table or desk during a TV interview. That's why actors plugging their films on talk shows bring clips or outtakes. These simple devices add visual interest to the television coverage, making stories come alive on the small screen.

HOW TO LOOK GOOD ON TV

When I say appearances count on television, I don't want to give the impression, as early practitioners of media training did, that appearances are all that count. Content counts, too. An energetic, attractive spokesperson who says nothing is delivering no message save that she is energetic and attractive.

However, appearance has unique impact in television interviews. An early — and historically significant — lesson in how much appearance counts on TV is the very first televised presidential debate in 1960. Vice President Richard M. Nixon eschewed makeup and so looked ghostly pale on the black-and-white screens of the era. He also sweated profusely — as was his wont throughout his career — and, not knowing where to look, Nixon glanced nervously from side to side. Conversely, Senator John F. Kennedy — guided by instinct or coaching or both — kept his gaze fixed on the moderator, Howard K. Smith. The senator used an orator's hand gestures to help him make his points, and seemed "tanned and fit," in part because of his sailing avocation and in part thanks to Max Factor theatrical makeup. As a result, people who watched the debate on TV awarded Kennedy a "win."

But the debate was simulcast on radio, and listeners — without the benefit of visual clues — thought the event was a draw, with Nixon delivering serious points in his deep, resonant voice, which contrasted with Kennedy's more reedy tones and his unusual Boston accent. The difference was cosmetic; on radio it didn't matter what Kennedy looked like but it did matter what he sounded like, while on television Nixon's pale and furtive appearance made him the loser.* While this may be a sad comment on the state of our democracy — that physical appearance matters more than content — it is the fact of the matter.

Despite the importance of the cosmetic side, just looking good is not enough. Your appearance won't overcome a lack of substance.

---

*While Kennedy looked "tanned and fit," we now know that he was, in fact, suffering from several serious ailments at the time and was in poorer health than Nixon, so his appearance was misleading.

Without paying eye service to the cosmetic demands of the medium, it is hard to convey your agenda points to viewers. Think of television's appearance requirements as the visual equivalent of a clear writing style. In print, dense, garbled sentences don't sell your ideas very well. You strive for clarity in written communication; you don't want the writing to get in the way of your thoughts. On television, your appearance and attitude are your visual style.

Here are eight simple wardrobe, appearance, and performance rules for television:

LOOKING GOOD ON TV

1. Dress Right
2. Sit Right
3. Stand Right
4. Move Right
5. Emote Right
6. Look Right
7. Talk Right
8. Leave Right

¶ **Dress right.** When he was president, Richard Nixon hosted my ABC News colleague, Gary Herman, and his cam-era crews for a photo-op "day of leisure" at his Western White House in San Clemente, CA. President Nixon decided to humanize his image and took his wife, Pat, for an on-camera walk along the beach. Characteristically, the President wore a dark business suit, a tie and lace-up black wingtip shoes. Had he been in a pair of Bermuda shorts and barefoot, the scene would have looked natural and charming, instead of staged and awkward. As ridiculous as the suit-on-the-beach stroll looked, it got worse when a higher than normal wave washed up on shore and the president did a little dance in a futile attempt to avoid getting his wingtips soaked. ABC News did Nixon the favor of not airing that particular bit of footage; showing the President of the United States walking on a beach in business attire was an odd enough visual even without the wave-dodging jig Nixon performed. Today, even if ABC News declined to air similar embarrassing footage, it would wind up on YouTube and then on all the nightly newscasts and, finally, on latenight comedy shows. Remember, the third and courth F words governing today's media are "Fame" and "Fun." That's a lesson Sen. John Kerry learned when he was running for President in 2004. Kerry visited NASA's Kennedy Space Center in Florida and, as required when visiting a NASA "clean room," donned a puffy white "clean suit." The problem was the suit made him look like he was auditioning to be the Easter bunny at a mall department store. The image was run repeatedly — and not just by news outlets. It even popped up in opposition print ads and commercials.

Remember the parental admonition: "You're going out dressed like that?" While it ought to be self-evident that a suit on a beach is as out of place as a pair of swim trunks in an office, there are gray areas of dressing for television. So before going on camera, imitate that parent and ask yourself, "You're going out dressed like that?" What should you wear? If business attire is correct for the occasion and for your position, men should wear a dark blue or gray suit without a pattern; women should wear a suit or daytime dress with the same color considerations. Avoid brown suits. President Ronald Reagan was partial to a particular brown suit, which he wore quite frequently. Under certain TV lighting conditions the suit looked reddish, almost the color of rust. I always found it distracting and wondered why someone as camera-savvy as Reagan wore it.

Wear a solid color shirt or blouse — pale blue is best — and avoid bright colors, striped shirts, ties and scarves. Also, wear lightweight clothing. While television lighting has come a long way since Nixon poured sweat during that initial 1960 debate and modern studios are much cooler, TV lights still are bright, and they generate heat, so dress accordingly.

Men should wear over-the-calf socks, so we don't see a slash of exposed flesh between trouser cuff and sock top. Women should avoid overly short skirts; oftentimes you will be seated on a very low chair — with all the hazards that represents. Minimize displays of jewelry — avoid any dangling necklaces that might hit your microphone. Also, if you're wearing a diamond the size of the Rock of Gibraltar on your finger, on your wrist, or around your neck, the chances are pretty good you're not going to connect with the average woman in the audience who could feed her family for a year or more for the price of that stone. The same goes for men's bejeweled pinkie rings and dia-mond-encrusted wristwatches. When I was supervising producer of ABC-TV's "Home Show," a new co-host joined the cast. She wore a blinding, large engagement ring. I suggested that she might want to take it off while she was on the air. "Who's going to see it?" she asked, declining my suggestion. The answer to her question was, "Every woman in the audience." When she did her first cooking segment and plopped her hand, adorned with eight or ten carats of flashing diamond, into the pizza dough, it provoked more than a few letters and faxes from view-ers offended by her ostentatious display of affluence. Today, with email communication available, the outpouring would have been far greater.

If business attire is not appropriate, you should still be dressed neatly, in subdued colors and no stripes. Obviously, if you are the fire boss fighting a blaze in a national forest or a squad leader in a combat zone, neatness does not matter. Avoid shirts and jackets with a designer logo or a lot of printing on them; you want viewers to be watching you, not trying to read your clothing. The only exception to the logo rule is your own company or organization logo. Then it is merely reinforcing your on-screen identification. In our security-minded world, many businesses and organizations require employees to wear ID tags or badges. Remove these before an interview; they can cre-ate annoying reflections and more than a few viewers will dis-tract themselves by trying to read your ID while you're talking.

¶ **Sit right.** Your mother was right: sit up straight in your chair. If you've watched interviews with sullen young stars of the music and acting worlds, you know why. Often, they sit on their necks, legs splayed in a wide V and invite your attention to their crotches instead of their faces. Don't copy them; sit the way the Victorians did: perched on the forward two-thirds of the chair, your back not even touching the seat back. It's a good idea to lean in slightly toward the interviewer. When you do, your body language says you are eager to talk with him, and the view-er assumes you are just as eager to communicate with her, too. Leaning back sends the opposite body language signal — you are physically retreating from the interviewer and from the view-er. An added benefit: when you sit upright you engage your core muscles, adding power to your voice and reminding you that you're not having a casual conversation.

Don't fidget! Once again, mom was right. A lot of us channel our nervous energy through our legs. We bounce our knees or drum our foot or — when we are in a chair that swivels — we do a seated version of the old rock and roll dance favorite, the twist. If you plant your feet solidly on the floor, imagining your heels glued to the deck, then it is nearly impossible to drum feet, bounce knees, or swivel your chair. It is a mystery to me why some TV shows furnish interview sets with soft, deep-cushioned sofas or swivel chairs, but they do, so exercise care: don't allow yourself to sink too deeply into the upholstery or swivel dizzyingly in your chair.

¶ **Stand right.** Standing interviews tend to be shorter than seated interviews, in no small part because the interviewer is as uncomfortable standing up as you are. Stand up straight; don't slump, but never lock your knees because a lack of blood circulation could cause you to pass out, and lying dazed on the floor is not an effective way to communicate your messages. Stand with your feet about shoulder width apart. This will keep you from rocking from side to side. And, please, keep your hands out of your pockets, it does *not* make you look cool.

SITTING OR STANDING, AVOID THE CUPP

Former Pres. Bill Clinton and former Sen. Bob Dole demonstrate the CUPP, or Cover Up Private Parts position. The CUPP sends a highly-defensive body language message.

I took the CUPP photo on Page 94 in March 2003, when Clinton and Dole appeared together on the "CBS Early Show." Throughout the five-minute segment, both men sat in the CUPP pose. I found it ironic that a president whose term in office was tainted by a sex scandal and a senator whose first private sector job was as a commercial spokesman for Viagra would adopt that particular defensive posture. (In fairness, Sen. Dole's World War II wounds left his right arm paralyzed so he frequently supports that limb with his left hand.) The anonymous man on the cover of this book is also cupping.

¶ **Move right.** Be expressive. Talk with your head, shoulders, and hands. This will give you energy and animation. Why do singers use hand gestures? Why do actors use their hands while delivering dialog? For three excellent reasons:

1. Using your hands helps you make a point. When a singer belts out a lyric about love, she often clutches her hands to her heart and then thrusts them wide. The gestures are helping her tell the story of the song. Similarly, when you say, "This is the biggest thing that's ever happened to our company" and you spread your arms in a modified "Soooo big" gesture, you're reinforcing the point you're making. Additionally, gestures can help you remember. If I were on television right now, telling the viewer why it's important to use hand gestures, I would demonstrate the three points by ticking them off on my fingers. Not only do I reinforce the fact that there are three points, but I also remind *myself* that there are three points I must describe.

2. Gestures attract attention; they make you look active. In that first 1960 presidential debate, Kennedy dramatized his points with very deliberate, almost karate chop hand gestures. Nixon, for the most part, let his hands rest on the lectern in front of him. Kennedy was interesting to look at; his gestures helped him create his vibrant, energetic image. What was most interesting about Nixon's appearance was his unfortunate and unrelenting sweat.

3. Gestures help energize your voice. Again, look at singers. They gesture not only to illustrate their songs, they also do it to help them throw their voices to the last row of the highest balcony. For the interview subject, gestures have the added benefit of burning off the nervous energy that he might otherwise express with foot tapping or finger drumming.

A cautionary note: If hand gestures are totally foreign to your nature, skip them. Forcing yourself to gesticulate unnaturally will divert important mental energy away from your Positive Message Statements. If you cannot gesture with ease, you are going to look like some sort of puppet when you force yourself to do it.

¶ **Emote right.** Some years ago, I was producing an interview with the spokesman for an automobile company. What he was saying was serious, the way he was saying it was not. Even though he was giving grim economic news, he had an idiotic grin smeared across his face as if he were doing a commercial for cosmetic dentistry. After a couple of moments, I called for a tape stop asked him why, when he was dealing with a negative story, he looked so happy.

"My media trainer told me I should always smile. It makes me look friendly," he said. And, I thought, it also makes you look indifferent to what you're saying. I suggested that "concerned" was more important than "friendly" in this case and he stopped grinning.

Since I wasn't in the room when he was trained, I can't testify about whether or not his account of the session was accurate. I hope not; media training like that gives our trade the same kind of reputation the medical profession gets from surgeons who leave retractors inside patients. Regardless of what the auto company spokesman may or may not have been told, it's important that your facial expression be appropriate to what you are saying. Go with your gut instincts on facial expressions; you know a big bright smile doesn't mesh with grim news and a mournful look fights an announcement of good news.

¶ **Look right.** In the movie "Get Shorty," John Travolta plays a kindhearted collector for mob loan sharks. His favorite line when intimidating a deadbeat is "Look at me." No threats, no strong-arm stuff, just, "Look at me." When you're doing a television interview, pretend that your interviewer is that character and has just intoned that instruction. Obey it.

You'll recall that Vice President Nixon had a tough time deciding where to look when he engaged Sen. Kennedy in that first debate. Consequently, he looked from side to side and forever earned a reputation for being shifty-eyed. It was such an enduring image that during the mad merchandising orgy that accompanied the Watergate scandal, a company put out a "Tricky Dick" watch adorned with a cartoon Nixon whose eyes shifted back and forth to tick off the seconds. It also contains his historic "I am not a crook" quote, making the watch a little media training treasure. I got one to film as part of a story I was doing on the business of Watergate and I kept it — as you can see, below — even though it stopped running decades ago.

So where do you look? Right in the interviewer's eyes. What if your reporter has an intense, unnerving hypnotic stare or, more commonly, is not looking at you but down in her lap where her list of prepared questions is resting? For the former condition, look at a spot on her forehead just above her eyes. For the lap-looker, direct your gaze at where her eyes would be if she were looking at you. Staring into someone else's lap is not a good idea on television.

Normally, I tell clients never to look in the camera unless they are doing a remote interview — in other words the interviewer is not in the room with them, but across town or across the country. In that case, treat the lens of the camera as if it were the interviewer's eye. A lot of people find it disconcerting to engage the wide glass eye of a television lens in conversation. If that's the case with you, write the interviewer's name on an index card and ask the cameraman to tape it just below the lens. The name will engage your eye and there's an added benefit: it reminds you of the reporter's identity and prompts you to use his name in some answers ("Well, Anderson, we are ready for the storm….").

There is one other exception to the rule of not engaging the camera. It needs to be used sparingly, judiciously and only by certain spokespersons. You may look into the lens of the camera during a face-to-face interview when you want to share a moment directly with viewers. Pulling your attention away from the interviewer and staring down the barrel of the lens can be extremely jarring so do it with great care and never more than once during an interview. And, if you're going to do it, then *do* it. Don't start talking toward the lens and then turn back to your interrogator before you finish the thought; that destroys the effect. Only the most practiced and confident spokespersons should try this direct-to-viewer move; this is not a trick for a novice.

¶ **Talk right.** As I indicated in Chapter 3, talking to the media is different from talking to your colleagues. An interview is a performance, not a conversation. Banish jargon and create verbal headlines for your Positive Message Statements. Lead with your strongest stuff; get that key point up front. Keep answers short and simple and use grabbers to capture a viewer's attention. Inject energy into your voice; if you don't sound interested in what you're talking about, the viewer won't be interested, either. Energy is *not* speed. You don't want to talk so fast that you outpace the listeners' ability to follow your ideas. Additionally, you need to know when to stop talking. You'll want to learn to talk right in four different circumstances: during the warmup, whenever there is a microphone present, when you are doing a mic check, and during the actual interview. Let's review each circumstance:

1. Talk right in the warmup In the last chapter, I covered the hazards of the warmup gaffe of saying to your interviewer — or anyone who might pass it on to your interviewer — "Gosh, I hope you aren't going to ask me about XYZ." Saying something like that is a virtual guarantee that "Tell me about XYZ?" will be the first question out of the reporter's mouth when the camera rolls. But this doesn't mean you shouldn't talk at all before your interview. In fact, you should talk about your PMSs in the warmup. Just as "Don't ask me about XYZ" sets the stage for a question about XYZ, so, "You know this new asthma medication has enabled youngsters who previously were housebound to actually go out and join little league teams," sets the stage for this question: "I've heard that this new medication has radically improved the lives of some youngsters. Can you tell me about that?" The interviewer, armed beforehand with the little league specific, is soliciting that story from you.

Just be sure you remember your own material. In the Green Room before an interview in connection with a novel I'd written, I joked to the host of a local New York talk show, "When I was a foreign correspondent in Rome and Berlin in the 1960s, I was so poor that I couldn't afford a trench coat; I had an umbrella instead." On air, John Bartholomew Tucker, the host, asked,"Working in Rome sounds pretty glamorous, but I guess it didn't pay very well?" He was trying to elicit my umbrella line, but I had forgotten my own quip and replied, "That's right. I worked for a very tightfisted newspaper." Tucker tried to save the gag. "So, you didn't have a trench coat?" I looked at him blankly. "What did you have?" he asked, pleading with me to remember. I did: "An umbrella?" My response was tentative, as if I was answering a quiz show question with a haphazard guess. He laughed dutifully, even though I'd blown my own joke.

2. Talk right if there's a microphone present. Treat a microphone like a gun. Just as we are taught to treat all guns at all times as if they are loaded, all microphones should be treated as if they always are on and recording or broadcasting. Never say anything near a microphone that you don't want the whole world to hear. An object lesson cited by every media coach in the country is Uncle Don. It seems Uncle Don had a popular kiddie radio show in the 1940s. One Friday he signed off, paused, and then said to his studio crew, "That ought to hold the little bastards for the weekend." The microphone was on, the studio was feeding audio to the air, and the little bastards — as well as many of the little bastards' parents — heard the remark and Uncle Don was fired.

Great story! The only problem is, it didn't happen. The Uncle Don story is completely apocryphal. There was, indeed, an Uncle Don on radio in New York during the 1930s and 1940s, but if he ever referred to his listeners as little bastards, it did not go out over the air. Much as I hate to lose Uncle Don as an object lesson, I still have George W. Bush, Barack Obama, Joe Biden, and Ronald Reagan to replace him.

When he was running for the Presidency in 2000, former Governor Bush spotted a New York Times reporter in the crowd at a Labor Day rally and whispered to his running mate, Dick Cheney, "There's Adam Clymer, a real major league @##%*!^

from the New York Times." There was a live microphone in front of Bush and the comment reverberated around the rally like a stadium announcer introducing a pitching change.

President Obama, meeting then Russian Federation President Medvedev in Seoul, South Korea in March of 2012, asked Medvedev to pass on a message to incoming Russian President Putin: "On all these issues, but particularly missile defense, this can be solved. But it's important for him to give me space....This is my last election. After my election, I have more flexibility." That private moment wasn't so private — a hot microphone right in front of the two Presidents picked up every word.

And who can forget Vice President Joe Biden whispering at the Affordable Care Act signing ceremony on March 23, 2010, "This is a big *&$#+@# deal." There is no such thing as a whisper when you do it in front of an open microphone.

In the annals of those who should know better, Ronald Reagan, takes the open microphone cake because he made his faux pas as part of a microphone check. Which bring us to:

3. Talk right in a mic check. Before his weekly radio address one Saturday morning, President Reagan was asked for a mic check. Instead of counting from one to ten — or, as rocket scientists do, from ten to one — the President decided to be funny. "Well," he said, "I've just declared war on Russia and the bombers are on their way." The remark did not go out live over the air. But the journalists assembled to cover his weekly address heard it, and they reported it. Why? Probably each reporter feared his competitors would go with the story, so each one defensively wrote it to avoid being scooped. Once the story moved on the newswires, radio stations across the country — which had recorded the joke because they had been rolling tape to capture the president's address — felt free to air it. And they did. Repeatedly. We can argue from now until the cows come home about the sanctity of the private jokes of a public man, but the fact of the matter is President Reagan — who began his working life as a radio announcer — should have been aware of the consequences of that mic check. Remarkably, despite the "war on Russia" embarrassment, Reagan did it *again*! Before another Saturday radio address his microphone check consisted of slamming the rulers of Communist Poland, calling them a "bunch of no-good, dirty bums."

Make better use of your mic checks than President Reagan; a mic check can be very productive. Instead of counting or reciting Lincoln's Gettysburg address when you're asked for a mic check, use the opportunity to state your name, your title, and a topic sentence to help set the agenda. If you do that, no interviewer will ever have an excuse for mispronouncing your name or for not knowing your title. And your topic sentence may well generate a question early in the interview.

Here's a sample mic check: "I'm Captain Picard, commander of the Starship *Enterprise* and I'm here today to tell you why we must defeat the Klingons." Having set that thought in an interviewer's mind, it is likely the first question will be, "Captain Piccard, why do you feel we must defeat the Klingons?" Even if he doesn't ask that, he's certainly not going to mistakenly call you Captain Kirk.

4. Talk right in the interview. Use the interviewer's first name — that's how the viewers know your questioner. It's Diane, not Ms. Sawyer; it's Anderson, not Mr. Cooper. This is an *American* rule; check local custom before doing it in interviews with foreign outlets such as Britain's BBC, France's ORTF or Germany's RTL. "Well, Bob…." Is more than just a friendly gesture, it buys you some milliseconds to organize your response without appearing to be stalling. Compare that with the old chestnut "I'm glad you asked me that question" or the never-to-be-employed "That's a good question." Either one of these statements is likely to unleash the aggressive beast in even the most passive house pet of an interviewer. Broadcast reporters and hosts don't want their audiences to think of them as fawning fans — even when they are fawning fans. So telling one of them in front of those viewers that, in effect, he has given you a "pass go, collect $200" softball may result in a daunting barrage of much tougher questions.

Avoiding verbal Tics. An important part of talking right is avoiding verbal tics such as "like," "y'now," "actually," and the almost universally-misused "literally." Generally these are habits or manifestations of nerves. If they are habits, they are harder to address because we may not even be aware we are letting them slip, y'know, into our, like, sentences. I have found the best way to avoid verbal tics is to demonstrate their harm and the best way to do that is to play back a practice interview and pause the video every time one of them slips out. Stopping for each tick will make you aware of how damaging they are to the flow of your ideas. For "like" and "y'know," I have another technique, but be aware that this will either cure it or make it profoundly worse. The technique: repeat the offending word or phrase rapidly for 30 seconds immediately before doing the interview. "Y'know, y'know, y'know, y'now…" repeated for a half-minute is going to have one of two results: you will be so aware of your penchant for using the term you'll banish it, or you will have planted it so firmly in your brain you won't be able to avoid it. Try this technique in a practice interview to see if in your case it is a cure or a killer. Insofar as "literally" is concerned, it is almost always used in place of the more accurate "figuratively." Make every effort to ban it. "Actually" is unnecessary nearly 100 percent of the time and in many businesses (especially show business) it means the opposite of its dictionary definition. "He's actually in a meeting," means he's not in a meeting. "He's actually at lunch," means he is, in point of fact, sitting at his desk shaking his head, "no," because he does not want to talk to you. The interview listener, hearing you protesting the accuracy of your answer by repeatedly inserting "actually," begins to doubt your veracity. (Actually begins to doubt your veracity?)

¶ **Leave right.** Parting may or may not be, in Shakespeare's words "sweet sorrow," but leaving a televised interview the wrong way can give you bitter sorrow. Don't heave a sigh of relief, as if the dentist has just withdrawn his probes from your mouth and freed you from his chair. Chances are better than even the audience will see it, and that gesture will undo much of the good you may have accomplished. Don't leap up and run away. If the camera catches that flight — and Murphy's Law guarantees that it will — the action makes you look like a fugitive. Also, it's likely that there's a microphone attached to some piece of your clothing. If it's a hard-wired microphone you're going to tear your clothing, tear the microphone cord, or tear both. You should not bolt from the scene at the end of a print interview, either. A reporter may well characterize your exit in her story this way: "Obviously relieved, Mr. Goodhue raced from the site even though the interview had been conducted in his own office."

At the end of a TV interview, don't reach out to shake hands with the reporter. If he extends a hand, take it, but don't initiate the gesture. Most reporters are not expecting to have their hand shaken after an interview and may be so slow on the uptake that their body language undermines your gesture. If the interviewer offers his hand — even if he's guilty of assault with a series of deadly questions — take it and shake hands. Hemingway defined courage as "grace under pressure;" shaking hands with an interrogating bully will be perceived as courageous on your part.

Don't leave with a negative editorial comment. "Boy, you were tough on me," "Thank goodness that's over," or, "You never asked me about...." First of all, your microphone, still clipped to your clothing, may be transmitting. Second, that's not a good way to add information. The interview may be over but the information gathering isn't. If something has been left out of a television interview and you want to add it, tell your interviewer in a positive way. Rather than: "You forgot to ask me about..." try saying, "I probably should have told you ..." The former implies the interviewer didn't do her job, the latter has you taking responsibility and offering to be helpful with additional information. I have seen recorded interviews conclude and then the interview subject say something like, "You know I probably should have talked about...." Whereupon the reporter said, "Well, let's do a few more minutes so we can discuss that." Even live broadcasts afford some follow-up opportunity. I can recall a guest occasionally coming up with a good point after we had gone to commercial on "Good Morning America." If the point was of sufficient interest, David Hartman would work it in after the break, in a subsequent interview, or on another day, paraphrasing the information or using it as the basis for a question to another guest. It's not the best way to get your point across, but it's better than leaving it unspoken.

TELEVISION INTERVIEWERS: THE GOOD, THE BAD, BUT RARELY THE UGLY

A few words about television interviewers: More than any other breed of journalist, television reporters serve two agendas — getting information and looking good — and not necessarily in that order. By looking good, I don't mean they want to look like a movie idol or a soap opera star; rather I mean looking good in the viewers' eyes by being perceived favorably. This is understandable since television is a personality-driven business, television performers are ego-driven people, and most TV newsrooms are infected with the personality/ego virus. If you have any doubt about how personality-driven television news is, look at Today Show host Matt Lauer's $25 million-a-year contract with NBC News. (An amount, incidentally, that is $5 million higher than the entire Good Morning America budget the last year I was executive producer of that program.) The network hired a personality to *read* the news and do in-studio interviews for a sum that could have fielded 20 to 25 journalists to *cover* the news where it was happening. The conflict between looking good and gathering information wears many faces in television. Here are a few examples:

¶ The reporter wants to appear tough, seasoned, and uncompromising, but the interview subject/victim is really a pitiable character. The reporter dare not cross the line from inquisitor to bully, so he pulls back on his questioning.

¶ The reverse situation: the reporter wants to appear tough and goes only for the jugular despite knowing mitigating facts and circumstances. She tempers anything that will make her appear compromising. This tough stance can backfire on the reporter. I remember a CBS News correspondent who sat in for Diane Sawyer as anchor of the "CBS Morning News" when I was executive producer of that broadcast. She had a reputation for toughness and in an interview with a breast cancer survivor, she got inappropriately rough. In the control room we watched this hard-edged interview in appalled silence. I can only imagine what viewers thought of this woman's misguided hostility. Her attitude, which might have been appropriate with a toxic waste dumper, was misplaced dealing with a woman describing the anguish of a double mastectomy.

¶ The reporter wants to appear to be friendly and charming, so he tempers his questions. During the heyday of the dot-com boom, business reporters fell over themselves doing puffball interviews with executives of startup firms whose sole reason for being was to make money in an initial public offering. In the cold, hard light of the economic realities of today, you would have thought that a lot of the business reporters were paid press agents instead of impartial journalists. The same was true of many TV business reporters in the run-up to the 2007 crash. Years back I trained a youthful Silicone Valley entrepreneur and when I sharply challenged his assertion that his company would make money by "monetizing" the "community" of web surfers it was going to create, he said to me, "No one's going to ask me anything like that." I warned him he'd better prepare for the possibility that future interviews would contain questions like mine. But the truth of the matter was that in the fawning financial journalism community, it's likely that the toughest questions he faced were mine.

¶ The reporter wants to be "one of the guys." This is especially true in show business and sports interviews, where some reporters want a star's glitter to rub off on them. So instead of asking real questions, the interviewer becomes an "insider" and chats up the subject. Many of the interviews of movie and music stars consist of the reporter gushing all over the artist, praising her work, endorsing her projects, and then popping a mild, "how do you feel about that" sort of question at them.

Why should you care about TV reporters wanting to look good? Because if you can help the reporter achieve that goal while still serving your agenda, he will cut you a lot more slack than if you're not helping him look good.

A smart performer makes every television interview appear to be a conversation between best friends, and often just doing that is shield against embarrassing — or even substantive — questions. The stars who get beaten up by TV all the time are those who won't take a few moments to play the role of the reporter's buddy. Some interviewers in the show business and sports fields can be both buddy and tough; it is a delicate balancing act which Rona Barrett perfected when she was at "Good Morning America." Rona once asked Gregory Peck about his son's suicide, leaving the normally articulate actor momentarily speechless. Rona also asked the late Rock Hudson, who had closeted his homosexuality, about a prank involving someone sending hundreds of invitations to the wedding reception of Hudson and the actor Jim Nabors, who was also gay and closeted. Hudson, stunned by the question, stopped cold, took out a cigarette, lit it, inhaled deeply, and then quietly and gently said words to the effect, "I didn't think you would ask about that." Then he added, "I thought this was a vicious and hurtful thing and I can shrug it off, but it deeply hurt a very decent human being." It was an extremely memorable moment. Had Hudson considered Rona's depth of knowledge of show business, her insider contacts, and her essential toughness, he might have expected such a probing question.

For those of us who are spokespersons without marquee value, a little flattery can go a long, long way. Even those on-air reporters you would think had developed immunity to praise are suckers for a complement or a promotional boost. For instance, consider Barbara Walters. On the first night of her brief tenure as co-anchor with Harry Reasoner on the "ABC Evening News," Walters interviewed Egypt's President Anwar Sadat. Sadat was a master of the media and he took a shot at flattery by commenting on his interviewer's new million-dollar anchor contract, the very first seven-figure talent deal in the history of American television news. The subsequent interview was not terribly probing. Was there a cause and effect? It's hard to say, but it didn't hurt Sadat's cause to compliment his interviewer

I saw the late novelist Nora Ephron castigate the Washington press corps for writing or broadcasting puffball stories about President George W. Bush. To turn the reporters, she said, Bush "complimented them on their tie." Lest you think Ms. Ephron's satirical side was exaggerating, in 2006, during a presidential news conference, Bush complimented a CNN reporter on his "sharp suit" and another reporter on her choice of blouse. The questions that followed the sartorial compliments were not particularly tough.

Wardrobe compliments aside, what do you do with the tough, hard-nosed reporter who wants to kick you through five minutes of on-air time? Conventional flattery may not work. As I already noted, you should avoid beginning an answer to a tough reporter's questions with: "Gee, that's a good question" because the cliché is like flapping a red cape in a bull's face. The bull/reporter muses, "If he thinks that's a good question, I'd better toughen up." With this sort of reporter, you need to be more subtle. The reporter wants to appear knowledgeable and smart so play to that desire. Credit the intelligence, wisdom, insight, and research behind the questions. Rather than saying, "That's a good question," begin your answer with, "Your question shows you understand the issue, so no doubt you know...." And move on to one of your agenda points. In effect you are saying, "You know and I know and now we'll share it with the audience so it will know."

Understand that there are limits to this trick. Flattery is like cayenne pepper. A little goes a long way. Too much will burn you, so flatter, don't fawn.

GOING LIVE:
CHALLENGE OR OPPORTUNITY?

The upside of a live television interview is that it is live, done in real time, and broadcast as it happens so nothing can be edited. The downside of a live television interview is that it is live, done in real time, and broadcast as it happens so nothing can be edited. If you're unprepared, the lack of editing can be a daunting challenge. If your message to the viewer is distorted it will be because you distorted it. On the other hand if you are prepared, you've got total control over everything the viewer hears from you; no one is going to be able to alter what you say.

Here are some tips for live interviews:

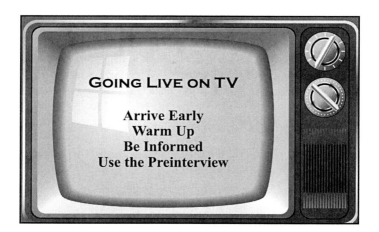

¶ **Arrive early.** Get to the studio fifteen minutes earlier than your call time. Even if the studio is your office and they've set up a remote link for you to talk to the interviewer at another location, get there early. An early arrival lets you take in the geography of the studio before the interview starts, lessening the danger of distraction. If it is a familiar place like your own office, the chances are the crew has rearranged some things, and you want to notice that *before* your interview, not in the middle of an answer. Another reason to arrive early, especially for a live interview: you won't sit down, breathless, have a microphone pinned on, and get your first question while you're hyperventilating.

You'd think a veteran television correspondent would be acutely aware of the importance of arriving early on the set of a live broadcast, but a particularly grievous late arrival involved a pro, the late Jules Bergman, ABC News' Science Editor. Some minutes before the launch of Apollo 11, the first moon landing mission, Jules absented himself from the anchor desk to find a restroom. As the clock ticked down toward air and the historic launch, staffers set out to find the long-absent Bergman so he could join cohost Frank Reynolds at the anchor desk. They found him strolling back from the distant bathroom, oblivious to the clock. When he realized how close airtime was, he began running, and he arrived at the anchor desk just in time to have his microphone pinned on. Then ABC was on the air. Bergman was sweating profusely and gasping so hard he could barely speak. Reynolds had to do all the talking until Bergman composed himself.

¶ **Warm up.** We've already dealt with the importance of the warmup in a previous chapter. But it's worth stressing here because it's most important to plant your PMS seeds before a live interview. The reason is simple: at the end of the interview, you won't get that classic "anything else we should know?" question. It just isn't done in live interviews. Moreover, since live interviews tend to be short and time is that much more precious, you want your interviewer to have strong clues about what you can talk about before you go on the air.

¶ **Be informed.** As important as it is to bone up on current events before any interview, it's doubly important before a live interview. There is no way to edit out your dumbfounded surprise when the interviewer prefaces a question with, "A little while ago, before we went on the air, your agency's budget was cut in half by the legislature." I have seen several spokespersons terminally embarrassed in live interviews by a reporter who had information that the spokesperson should have had.

¶ **Use the preinterview.** Many interview programs, especially the live or live-to-tape shows, have staff members pre-interview guests. They do this so that the on-camera interviewer has an advance idea of what a guest is likely to say. You should use the preinterview to stress your agenda points to the producer or booker. Chances are she will work them into the set of questions she supplies your interviewer. On more entertainment-oriented program like "The Late Show" or "The Tonight Show," these preinterviews are the building blocks for an entertaining segment. In these cases the writer may well suggest straight lines for you to deliver to the host or gag lines you can unleash when the host throws straight lines to you. This sort of interview is more about fun than fact, but a lot of preparation goes into them, giving you advance notice of where the questioning will go. Thus informed, you can also figure out how to work your message points into the segment. Always make yourself available for a preinterview. Some shows have a hard-and-fast rule that guests must submit to preinterviews or they are unbooked.

When I was executive producer of "Good Morning America," we routinely cancelled guests who were uncooperative about submitting to preinterviews. The only guests exempt from preinterviews were persons of extraordinarily high stature, like the president, cabinet members, or heads of state. Most of those high-ranking officials made available to us staff members who would stand in for their bosses in preinterviews. The preinterview gives you good insight into what the interviewer will ask on the air. Once at "Good Morning America" we were preparing for an interview with the nation's top spy, the DCI, Director of Central Intelligence, head of the CIA. He supplied us with an aide who we preinterviewed and then a group of us remained behind in a CIA conference room and discussed the flow of questions we would ask the director. I can't say for a fact that the room was bugged, but the next day before we did the interview, the DCI brought in a looseleaf briefing notebook that his staff had prepared. I was sitting opposite him at the table as he reviewed it and I managed to spy on the top spy, reading the notes upside down as he reviewed them (reading upside down is a skill most newspapermen master — something to keep in mind if your desk is littered with confidential documents). I read in his briefing book every question we had discussed the day before along with his staff's suggested responses. So my spying on the top U.S. spy revealed his spies had spied on us — a circle worthy of a John LeCarre′ novel. It will be extremely rare that you'll have the opportunity to bug your reporter. And, if you do somehow have the opportunity and avail yourself of it, you'll probably be committing a felony. However, you can often figure out from the preinterview many of the questions you'll be asked.

Television is a demanding medium but TV exposure is worth the challenges because it is attention-commanding and plays to far larger audiences than all but a handful of newspapers. Effective television communication skills translate well to other media and to daily communication as well. ABC's Diane Sawyer wrote that my rules for interviews "work for all of life. You can use them on TV, at meetings, on job interviews, on dates, or ordering a pizza by phone." I'm not too sure about the pizza ordering application, but in all other respects, I heartily agree.

There is one branch of the television tree that requires special attention and a great deal of care if you're ever asked to appear.   This is the investigative program, the hour-long news shows that have proliferated as networks seek inexpensive ways to fill airtime. The next chapter delves into how you can survive these daunting shows.

DIGGING DEEP:
INVESTIGATIVE BROADCASTS

Throughout this book I have urged you to regard media encounters as opportunities. I've counseled that preparation and attitude will see you though an interview and let you take control, that creating your own agenda and honing your message points will carry the day for you. Now it's time for "yes, but…;" the exception to those rules.

The investigative broadcasts like "60 Minutes," "20/20," "48 Hours," and the numerically-challenged "Dateline NBC," may present an opportunity all right — an opportunity to hang yourself in public. These shows are unlike any other media and they deserve separate consideration. When you're preparing for an interview on one of them, you'll need to deploy a singular strategy; and often it's a *survival* strategy.

When I was the executive producer of the "CBS Morning News," I would sometimes share a lunch table in the CBS Broadcast Center cafeteria with the late Don Hewitt, the creator and executive producer of "60 Minutes." Hewitt told me that his concept of "60 Minutes" was a prime time adventure show about the exploits of (at that time) five men who, like the iconic heroes of old western movies, rode into town and righted wrongs. Instead of U.S. marshals or Texas Rangers, these five cowboys happened to be newsmen. Hewett's on-screen "magnificent five" back then were Morley Safer, Dan Rather, Ed Bradley, Harry Reasoner, and Mike Wallace.

I'm telling you this so you'll understand that "60 Minutes" and its many imitators are not really fair, impartial renderings of fact. Rather, they are information-based entertainment vehicles, designed to excite an emotional response from viewers. To that end, broadcasting's investigative cowboys load their six-shooters with interview questions and shoot to kill. If you wind up appearing on one of these shows, you've got to be sure you don't give these gunslingers a juicy target.

What should you do when a producer for one of the investigative shows calls and invites you to submit to an interview?

Do you blow him off? Do you embrace the opportunity? Do you send a colleague into the jaws of hell? Well that depends on what role the producers have in mind for you.

ARE YOU A GOOD GUY OR A BAD GUY?

It is a rule of theater, movies, and scripted television that you cannot have drama without conflict. You cannot have conflict without at least two contending sides. On one side of the conflict is the hero. On the other side of the conflict is the villain. Good guys vs. bad guys. In the terminology of old western movies, white hats and black hats. So it is on the reality-based dramas presented on the investigative TV newsmagazine shows. When the friendly producer from one of these shows phones you to talk about a story, the first question to ask yourself is: "Am I a good guy or a bad guy?" There are no hard-and-fast rules for casting good and bad guys. Certain categories — environmentalists, justice-seekers, whistle-blowers, owners of small farms or ranches, mom and pop businesses menaced by big box stores, unjustly convicted prisoners — are usually white hats. Bankers, bullies, and billionaires, are usually black hats. Despite these general assignments, though, there are no pat answers as to who will be a bad guy and who will be a good guy in any specific segment of these shows.

"60 Minutes," in particular, revels in the unpredictable — frequently lionizing individuals or companies generally branded as bad guys and skewering some usually considered good guys. Just because you or your organization is usually praised by the rest of the press, there's no reason to assume one of these shows will join the bandwagon. In fact, the show may be trying to flatten the bandwagon's tires.

On the air, "60 Minutes" often gives us subtle visual clues about who is a bad guy and who is a good guy. In fact, you can sometimes tell one from the other with the sound muted! Everyone — save the show's expanding roster of aging talent — is recorded in a close-up. But bad guys are framed in *extreme* close-up and from a slightly lower angle. The show reserves the unflattering "up the nostrils" shot for the villains. Wider framing, shot from eye level or slightly above, is reserved for good guys. The other nonfiction drama shows don't go in for this visual gimmick, although they do like it if the bad guy sweats on camera. Another visual clue is B-roll of the correspondent strolling along, talking to an interview subject. Typically, correspondents stroll only with the good guys because the image tells the audience the correspondent is on his side, figuratively as well as literally.

Obviously, it's too late to prepare your defensive strategy if you learn you're the bad guy after they pin on a microphone and the camera starts shooting up your nostrils. So you must determine in advance whether you're going to be standing shoulder to shoulder with the news lawman or facing him across the O.K. Corral. A little later on in this chapter, I'll give you some tips for determining your role on an investigative show.

WHAT'S A GOOD GUY TO DO?

If you're confident that you're going to wear a white hat in this western, proceed with your interview preparation the same way you would any other interview. Ready your agenda PMSs and grabbers, anticipate questions you might get, practice your answers, determine to whom you're speaking — the show's audience — and study the outlet and the individual reporter's style. Do all that and you should be fine; in fact you should emerge not merely unscathed but enshrined. But that's only if you're a good guy.

WHAT'S A BAD GUY TO DO?

If you find Wyatt Earp and his brothers oiling their Colts and practicing their quick draws for a journalistic shoot-out with you, what's your move? Do you saddle up and ride out of town or do you stand up to them? Let me give you two case histories that are valid object lessons in dealing with investigative shows.

Case history I — blocking the story. A foreign-owned automobile company that assembled some of its cars in the United States brought me in to prepare some spokespersons for interviews on a network investigative newsmagazine show. A confidentiality agreement prevents me from revealing the company name and I've decided to also shield its nationality, so let's call them Quickcar Motors of Carland.

"What's the story," I asked.

Quickcar's U.S. publicity chief told me the show was going to do a story about the company's local plant using the same highly-robotic production techniques the firm pioneered in Carland.

I smelled a rat and asked him: "Have you ever seen that show do an industrial story? What are they *really* after? What controversies are brewing in your assembly plant?"

After several minutes of insisting that first of all, a network news producer wouldn't lie to him, and, second, the Quickcar production techniques *were* a great story, he admitted that some workers had been expressing grievances — unwarranted, he averred — about perceived on-the-job racial and gender bias.

Warranted or unwarranted, that's the story the show is after, I told him. The discrimination charge was an investigative story; it had conflict, good guys, bad guys. Building automobiles the Quickcar way had no conflict and no bad guys so it was an unlikely theme for a network investigative show.

He protested there no merit to the grievances. It didn't matter, I told him; Quickcar had long enjoyed glowing reviews for its products and a could-do-no-wrong reputation in the media. Thus is was just the type of big, brightly-lit window investigative reporters enjoy shattering with a well-aimed brick. My client's spokesperson could well have been blindsided with the discrimination accusations had he submitted to the interview without identifying the true purpose of the story. On camera, the unprepared spokesperson might well sputter and stammer defensively, ill-equipped to cite exculpatory statistics. It would have been guilt by appearance.

I urged the client to take the calculated risk of not supplying a spokesperson and not letting the show's cameras into the plant to videotape the assembly line. I figured that the story was so heavily dependent on production-line images and an on-camera bad guy, the show could not tell it without Quickcar's cooperation. I was right; the show dropped the story. You, too, may be able to block an unfavorable story by preventing it from being shot, so long as you understand what the real scoop is and what it will take in terms of footage for the broadcast to achieve its goal.

The biggest risk in my approach was that the show might position one of its reporters in front of the plant and record him saying something like, "They wouldn't let us in," using that fact as an indication of guilt. My calculation was that while the "locked out" stunt is advocacy journalism of a sort, it is just too visually lame to make a good network newsmagazine segment. Something like that works on a daily newscast, where the average story is less than two minutes long, but investigative magazine show segments are much longer and require point-counterpoint confrontations. Point-point with no counterpoint is bad drama when stretched over a 10-minute segment.

Case history II — emerging unscathed from the O.K. Corral. Not everyone can shut out the investigative shows. Public agencies, for example, often can't deny access even to the most aggressive journalists; so their spokespersons have to do the best they can to deny investigative predator/reporters anything to chew on.

A few years ago I prepared a government agency spokesman for an investigative segment on one of the network investigative shows. We knew he was going to be the bad guy. The segment was about a controversial government-sponsored endeavor, and because this one had a high visibility, the show's producer made no pretense about the report's subject when he called to book my client. I helped the spokesperson organize a number of defensive strategies. First, I suggested his public relations representative tell the show's producer that the agency was going to made a video recording of the interview. (I advocated *telling* the producer the agency was going to record the interview, not *asking* the producer's permission.) The TV producer couldn't very well say no, since he was going to have two cameras in the conference room where the interview was to take place. I recommend video archiving this type of show, not just audio recording, which is adequate for most interviews. Video will keep the show exceptionally honest because your omnipresent camera constantly reminds the reporter and producer they'd better deal ethically with your answers and not stick answer C after question A or engage in other editing trickery.

I recommend pointing the client's camera at the reporter, not at the spokesperson. Positioned that way, the client camera is likely to reduce reportorial theatrics. I'll have more on taping a potentially hostile interview later, but let me focus for now on the case at hand.

My client's investigative interview was an education in and of itself. In his forty-minute Q&A session, the reporter used every trick enumerated in "The Interviewer's Top Eight Dirty Tricks" in Chapter 4: he put words in the spokesman's mouth, he asked questions based on false or incorrect information, he assaulted the interviewee with deadly questions, using a tone more appropriate to a criminal court than to an interview. In addition, he asked hypothetical questions, he interrupted answers to throw the spokesman off-message, and he delivered long, hectoring preambles to questions. He indulged in false equivalencies, taking as fact baseless assertions of my client's enemies. Finally, there were a significant number of pregnant pauses, invitations for my client to break into jail. He also asked the same questions three, four, and five times, hoping that the spokesman would get so bored with his answers he would vary them and misspeak.

But my client had already been asked all those questions. Repeatedly. First by me, and then by his public relations department. Many intensive hours of mock hostile interviews enabled him to answer the tough questions and remain in control. In fact, his preparation allowed him to remain so calm and unemotional that he gave the program nothing to use: no embarrassing statements, no nervous stammering, no flashes of anger. In its finished report, the show didn't use one second of the interview they taped with him because my client refused to play his assigned role: the furtive bad guy exposed by the muckraking reporter. The show found another spokesman from the same agency and interviewed him. Unfortunately for my client, the new spokesman declined media training, was unprepared for the onslaught, and plummeted into a number of avoidable pitfalls. An added lesson: these shows are persistent so an organization must make sure that anyone who represents it in an encounter with one of them is adequately trained and prepared.

Through diligent preparation and a calm demeanor, you can maintain your cool and score points, no matter how hostile the reporter's intent. It is possible to not merely survive an encounter with "60 Minutes" and its brethren, but to use it to serve your own agenda.

GIRDING FOR BATTLE

Whether you're the good guy or the bad guy, there are seven specific rules of engagement to follow to make sure you are most effective in an investigative television interview.

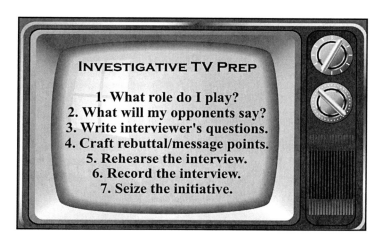

INVESTIGATIVE TV PREP

1. What role do I play?
2. What will my opponents say?
3. Write interviewer's questions.
4. Craft rebuttal/message points.
5. Rehearse the interview.
6. Record the interview.
7. Seize the initiative.

1. What role do I play? In the two case histories I've cited, one client did not know if he was the good or bad guy, and the other was sure he was the bad guy. Ask yourself the following questions to determine if you've been cast as the villain:

¶ **Were you a source when the show researched the story?** These investigative segments cost a lot to produce, so they don't just go out and shoot a story. If a TV newsmagazine tries to book you for an interview without having spoken to you at length beforehand, chances are they want to hear what you have to say only when the camera is rolling. In other words, the producers have already made up their minds about the story and your role in it. If you answered "No" to this question, chances are you're the bad guy.

¶ **Does the producer's description of his story sound like the sort of piece that the show normally airs?** If you answer "No," then he's misleading you about the real story. Only bad guys are misled.

¶ **In the preinterview, did the producer try to get you to comment off the record or were there echoes of the other side's ideas embedded in her questions or attitude?** If you answered "Yes," prepare for a hostile interview.

2. What will my opponents say? Try to learn who your opponents are. Ask the producer or reporter if he will email you a list of everyone else he will interview for the story and those he's spoken to in researching the story. If the producer tells you he doesn't know who else he'll be interviewing, he's not telling the truth. If he does send a list and obvious adversaries are not on it, be suspicious, you're probably being cast as a bad guy. Make your own list of opponents, if you decide to go through with the interview this will be useful.

Here's an offensive tip: Whether or not you get a list, write the producer recommending additional people to interview. These should be individuals unaffiliated with your enterprise who agree with your point of view. Your recommendations may be ignored, but if they are not, you've given them leads that will buttress your side.

Using either the producer's list, if you get one, or your own list — or both — create a sheet with the points you anticipate your opponents will make. Visit opposition web sites, read their posts. Be prepared to answer their specific charges with specific rebuttals. Put yourself into your opponent's head. Ask yourself what she will have told the producer or reporter off-camera to entice him to do this story. Remember, the more sensational the charge, the more attractive it is to the producer, so don't hold back, even if your opponent's assertions are preposterous! Prepare your list on a computer so you can cut, paste, and insert your rebuttal material.

3. Write the interviewer's questions. Below each of your opponent's points write a tough, hostile question derived from that point. Don't be diplomatic or shy. Make the questions pointed, direct, and stinging. If you're prepared for the tough questions, you can handle the easy ones. If you're prepared only for the easy questions, the tough ones will throw you.

4. Craft Rebuttal/Message Points. After you've written out all the hostile questions an interviewer might ask, insert a counterargument for each question. Do this right into your document immediately after the tough question. It is not enough merely to defend yourself in these situations because you don't want to appear to be fighting a rearguard action. Your counterargument answer/points should be strong, positive expressions of your side of the issue. And remember the rule of three — it takes three positive points to overwhelm a single negative. Here is a concrete example of the rule of three. In media training for NASA someone always comes up with some variation of this tough question: "Why spend money on space exploration when there are such pressing needs here on earth?" Generally, this is followed by a specific terrestrial problem like disease, hunger, poverty, inferior education, or environmental degradation.

NASA spokespersons needed to come up with three positives, a shock and awe response. Over the years, participants in my NASA media training workshops have supplied me with an embarrassment of riches in response to that question. Merging multiple effective responses, I found that not only are there three cogent rebuttal points, but the last point has a subset of three more points. Here are the elements of that response:

1. NASA's budget is approved by the people's representatives in Congress.
2. NASA's budget is less than one half of one percent of the total federal budget.
3. NASA's budget is an *investment* that pays society a variety of beneficial dividends.

The dividends — in a series of three — are:
1. NASA creates science and technology jobs; the kind of jobs America needs in order to stay competitive in an increasingly technology-driven world economy.
2. NASA's missions have broadened knowledge of our planet, our solar system and our universe. In fact they have rewritten astronomy and physics textbooks.
3. Spinoffs of technologies developed by and for NASA have improved our daily lives by enabling powerful computer microprocessors, by giving us global positioning satellites, by supplying life-saving accurate weather predictions and by enabling medical imaging devices that give early warning of cancers and other deadly diseases.

This three-part answer, with its three-part subset is a shock and awe response to the negative "waste" or "spend" money on space. For media purposes we can't get all of this to fit our ideal soundbite length of 30 words, spoken in ten seconds and comprised of three sentences. But with some condensation, here is a soundbite version:

"NASA's budget, under one percent of federal expenditures, invests in high-tech jobs; knowledge of earth's place in the universe, and spin-offs that make our lives easier and healthier. [Twenty-eight words if you count the hyphenated high-tech and spin-offs as a single word, 30 words if you count them as two words.]

Following up on the soundbite portion, the respondent can cite specifics.

5. Rehearse the Interview. Get someone to throw your tough questions at you in a confrontational and challenging manner. If your questioner is a subordinate, assure him you won't hold his demeanor against him. Don't try to question yourself. Even if you have a strong masochistic streak, you're not going to be tough enough.

Have your interrogator get aggressive, even antagonistic; have him ask the same question repeatedly. Have your colleague read the interviewer's dirty tricks in Chapter 4 before he grills you. Record the session, watch it, and analyze your performance. Then do it again. And again. Do it until you are almost comfortable under the withering fire of hostile question-ing; until you have learned to ignore the tone of a question and to answer only the substance of the question.

You want to get accustomed to building bridges from tough questions to your rebuttal points. Remember the lesson of Chapter 4: it's often easier to bridge from a tough, hostile question to a PMS than it is to navigate from a friendly, but off-the-point query. Make sure you don't look too programmed; remember it's a *television* interview and the audience can see your face, so you don't want to look and sound like a robot repeating canned answers. You need to be so familiar with your material that you can take advantage of any opportunity to score your rebuttal points, and you want to do it with grace and a degree of dignity.

When you review the video of your practice interviews, critique yourself mercilessly. Then repeat the exercise. Count the rebuttal points you are able to work into the interview. If you had five points to make, repeat the exercise until you are adept at getting all five points into the practice interview. Let that exercise interview run long; remember these investigative shows may interview you for as long as, well, sixty minutes. They may have at you for that long in hopes you'll hang yourself with a single incriminating ten-second soundbite. It's better to have a colleague beat you up with these questions in the privacy of your own office than to have Steve Kroft do it on "60 Minutes" with the whole world watching. Kroft, interviewed on CBS's "The Early Show" said, "We always know the answers to the questions before we ask them." That's hyperbole; Kroft and his colleagues don't really know what the answers will be before they ask their questions, but they certainly know that they *want* the answers to be. If you don't play along and give them the anticipated answer, the investigative correspondent will probably keep asking that question, hoping you'll eventually respond with the answer he wants. Practice can keep you from falling into that trap!

6. Record the Interview. As I suggested earlier, record the investigative TV interview on video, letting the reporter and producer know you're doing it. It does you less good to have a spycam somewhere in your office than it does to let them see you are archiving the interview. Be aware that it's illegal in 13 states and the District of Columbia to clandestinely record another person and it's of dubious morality even where it's legal. Taping an interview keeps the interviewer honest: he won't be tempted to carve up your answers to the point of distorting your position and he certainly won't put answer B to question A. By focusing your camera on the interviewer, you're going to minimize the brow furrowing, the intense staring, and the other theatrics that are the stock in trade of investigative interviewers.

7. Seize the Initiative. If you think your interview has gone badly and you feel a disastrous report will be aired, take the initiative and get out in front of the story. These newsmagazine broadcasts can't move as fast as a daily news show or a newspaper, so mobilize your organization's publicity apparatus to get the story out to the public before the investigative story airs. Tell the story from your point of view and tell it with as much fanfare as you can.

THE INVESTIGATIVE INTERVIEW

In the investigative interview, all the rules of TV interviews apply. Read the papers, listen to newscasts, and check online news sources immediately before your interview. You don't want to be caught flat-footed, ignorant of late-breaking developments. Check opponents' web and social media sites; they may have posted their most recent accusations there; charges which may inform the reporter's questions. And review this recap of key TV interview tips:

¶ **Arrive early.** Even if the interview is in your own office, be there while the crew is setting up; that way you won't be distracted once the interview starts.

¶ **Eat something.** You don't want your blood sugar level falling during an interview. Avoid alcohol, dairy products and caffeine — alcohol does not calm you, it lulls you; milk, cream and other dairy products produce phlegm, which can make your voice very unattractive, and caffeine can make you hyperactive.

¶ **Greet and chat with the producer and correspondent**. Under normal circumstances it is tougher for a reporter to beat up someone she feels she knows, but investigative reporters are generally immune to this sentiment. Still, chatting in advance doesn't do any harm so long as you don't get lulled into a false sense of security by the reporter's or producer's friendly attitude. Use the warmup to suggest the message points you want to work into the interview.

¶ **Expect the worst.** Normally, you would go into an interview expecting that *perhaps* there will be some tough questions. In an investigative TV interview, tough questions are guaranteed; even good guys sometimes get hit with them. If you are the black hat you're going to experience every one of the interviewer's eight dirty tricks listed in Chapter 4 and you're going to get them repeatedly. The pregnant pause, the words in your mouth, the misrepresentation of your words, the out-of-left-field hypotheticals, and the accusatory tone — all these will come at you time and again.

Don't let a reporter's tricks throw you. He will hammer away with them to shake your composure and get you to move off-message or to get you to appear defensive. Stick to your answers, don't change your message points for the sake of change, don't waver from your rebuttal points, don't compromise, and don't let the interviewer pressure you into retreating. Above all, remain calm, composed, unshakable, and positive — and, despite the repeated assaults with deadly questions, stay friendly. The reporter knows that if he gets too hostile with someone who remains reasonable and friendly, he's the one who will lose the audience's sympathy. A final reminder on the pause: in this type of interview, do *not* take advantage of a reporter's pause in the questioning. Normally, when a reporter stops he is searching for a next question and it's a good time for you to insert a message. In an investigative or hostile interview, the pause is a trick to get you to expand on an answer you've already given, to go beyond what you really want to say, to break into jail.

POSTINTERVIEW

When the interview ends, don't beat a hasty retreat from the scene. Instead, stick around while the crew packs up, and act as if there are no hard feelings — even if there are. Feel free to suggest additional rebuttal points, other people the interviewer can speak to, and other research material he might consult. Keep your discussion on point and positive. Don't volunteer anything negative; it could wind up in the completed story with or without attribution to you.

If, after looking at your video of the interview, you discover that there are valid rebuttal points you failed to make, email them immediately to the correspondent, with copies to his producer and executive producer. At the very least, they are ethically bound to consider these points for inclusion into the finished piece and you will be on record as having proffered them.

Also, take the time to analyze the video and critique how you answered the questions. A thorough review will help you to avoid any mistakes and to repeat any triumphs in future interviews. If others who share your point of view will be interviewed in the future, give them a heads-up warning about what they're likely to face.

BEATEN UP AND BLOODIED, BUT NOT DEFEATED

If the story airs and seriously misrepresents you or your organization, resist the temptation to sit quietly by, licking your wounds. Complain to everyone and anyone who will listen. Show your video of the interview to TV critics, journalism professors, even to local affiliates of the network that misrepresented you. Send video copies of the interview and an air check of the broadcast to all these people and to the president of the offending news division and to his network bosses as well. A word of warning: do this only if the misrepresentation is serious, not simply because you've got a bruised ego or because you misspoke on camera. Don't complain if the investigative show got it right, as ARAMCO did about one of my investigative pieces.

In 1973, during the Arabian oil embargo, an executive of the Arabian/American Oil Company — ARAMCO — complained to the president of ABC TV about a segment I produced. The executive claimed we'd misrepresented him when we showed him saying that, although at the time ARAMCO was a publicly traded American corporation, he owed his first loyalty to "his majesty the King of Saudi Arabia." When we filmed the interview, the answer surprised us, so the reporter, David Schoumacher, asked the question again. And again. The executive had three chances to give a different answer, perhaps one that mentioned ARAMCO's American stockholders. But he never availed himself of the opportunity.

The ABC president screened the entire interview I had shot then said, "I can see why he's upset, but he not only said it, he said it three times. He should have thought about how it would look before he opened his mouth, not after we aired it. And he might have gotten rid of that flag, while he was at it." (Visible in our wide shot was a small Saudi flag on the executive's desk. The flag features a sword — not the friendliest symbol to show Americans in those troubled times.)

Appearing on an investigative television news program, can be extremely intimidating. Two similarly daunting media experiences are the ambush interview and the shoutfest. I'll cover both in the next chapter.

BUSHWHACKED: SURVIVING AN AMBUSH; WINNING A SHOUTFEST

Two of the media's biggest challenges are the TV ambush and the broadcast shoutfest. While they are very different experiences, they share two characteristics: neither is pleasant and neither is conducive to expressing your agenda. Ambush interviewers catch you unprepared; you get no warning and you are without an interview agenda. In a shoutfest, you'll go into the studio with an agenda, but the challenge is making that agenda heard over the competing roar of other guests. You can survive an ambush and you may be able to get a few points into even the windiest of shoutfests. Here's how:

AMBUSH INTERVIEWS

TV ambushes are commonplace because they can deliver good, dramatic video. We've all seen them: crusading journalists accosting furtive interview subjects with little to say and much to hide. That's all an ambush is: an aggressive reporter accosting an unsuspecting — and often unwilling — interview subject in an unexpected location and throwing a succession of questions at him.

If you don't answer a print reporter's ambush questions, he is likely to write, "Mr. Richards refused comment." Or "Confronted with questions outside his office, Mr. Richards declined to comment for this article." That's a lot less damaging to Mr. Richards than the television depiction of that same refusal to talk; especially if Mr. Richards runs away. What could be better theater than video of a corporate executive fleeing a reporter? The image is a visual *nolo contrendre* plea to any charge the reporter has made.

In an ambush there are no niceties, no "Good afternoon, sir, may we ask you a few questions." There is just the challenging first question, usually shouted at top volume, and, if the bushwhackee doesn't answer instantly, several more rapid-fire questions, often without time between them for an answer.

What should you do if you suddenly find yourself in this situation? First, don't run away! Stand your ground and talk to the reporter. Before getting into what you *should* say, let Dan Rather show you what *not* to say. Rather, then at CBS, was confronted on the street outside his office. The perpetrator of the Rather ambush was Steve Wilson, an aggressive investigative reporter then working on a syndicated daily newsmagazine show. The supreme irony was that Wilson's ambush of Rather was a direct outgrowth of a failed ambush by Rather.

Months earlier, Rather had done a "60 Minutes" story about a storefront physician in Los Angeles who, the program contended, was faking injury reports in an insurance fraud scheme. With two video crews, Rather accosted the doctor in the parking lot of his clinic. The doctor ran away from Rather. But he had a still camera with him and every few steps, he turned around and snapped some shots of Rather and one of the "60 Minutes" crews. The other crew recorded a wide shot of the whole bizarre episode.

It turned out Rather had the wrong man; his prey with the camera was *not* the doctor. Naturally, the sequence wasn't used in the "60 Minutes" story. When the real doctor sued the network for libel, his lawyers sought all the film shot for the report as trail evidence. For unfathomable reasons, CBS's attorneys departed from normal practice and did not object to the introduction into evidence of the unused portion of the film, the "outtakes."

At the time, I was executive producer of "Entertainment Tonight," and our very enterprising reporter covering the story, Scott Osborne, asked the judge whether or not the outtakes — as evidence — weren't public record. The judge agreed and turned over the outtakes to Osborne. "Entertainment Tonight" ran a story about the case featuring CBS's footage of the misguided ambush. In the wake of our report, Steve Wilson, who worked for another syndicated show, staked out the CBS Broadcast Center on West 57th Street in New York, planning to ambush Rather. When Rather emerged from the building, Wilson and his crew struck, ambushing the ambusher. Wilson popped a tough question at Rather who stopped in his tracks. "Bring that thing up here," the CBS newsman said, indicating the microphone. "You hearing me pretty good?" Rather asked Wilson's audio operator. The man nodded. Rather got really close to the mic "Well," he resonated, "@%&*you. You got that?" And in case there was any doubt, Rather repeated himself, "@%&* you. Now you got that, right?"

Wilson was speechless and Rather walked away, no doubt confident Wilson had nothing he could broadcast. Like President Reagan with his attempt at humor during a microphone check, Rather should have known better. Not only did Wilson's show air a report on the encounter (with the expletive bleeped but clearly discernible to anyone who had gotten beyond the fourth grade), but they made a copy of the tape available to "Entertainment Tonight" and we ran it, too.

Now you're probably asking, "If I don't take flight and if I don't unleash my expletive vocabulary, what am I to do if I'm ambushed by a TV reporter?" I have two hard-and-fast rules for surviving an ambush interview:

Rule 1: Don't run away. If you flee, you will appear to be — and, in fact, you will be — a fugitive from the newsman and the public.

Rule 2: Don't reward an ambusher with an interview. Granting an ambush artist a spontaneous interview is a losing proposition; you need to get out of the ambush situation and buy yourself some time to figure out what the interviewer's story is and what you want to say. To do this, calmly tell the reporter, "I'd like to help you with your story, but since we don't have an appointment and I can't spare the time for you right now, if you call my office, we'll set something up and we can sit down and do a real interview."

Other perfectly plausible reasons for postponing an ambush include:

¶ "I'm not really current on the subject and I don't want to speculate or give misleading information. Let me find out more about it and get back to you and we can set something up so your viewers get the full story."

¶ "Company policy prohibits talking to the media about a case that's in litigation, and since this matter is a subject of litigation, I'm afraid all I can say is that the courts will decide the matter on its legal merits." (Obviously, you use this only when the ambush pertains to a case in litigation.)

¶ "The judge hearing this case has imposed a gag order on any potential witness. Since there's a possibility I may be called, if I speak to you I would be violating that order and face contempt of court charges. So until the gag order is lifted, I'm afraid

I can't discuss this at all." (Use this only when there is such a judicial order.)

Notice in the first two instances, you've stated a desire to help the reporter and have invited him to call you for an appointment. His response will likely be to shout more questions or even make threats such as, "Well, we're going to have to go without your side of the story." Remain calm and steadfast, *don't* be intimidated by this tactic. Give him nothing more than, "I'm sorry you feel the need to go ahead with your story without complete information, but I've explained that I'm willing to talk to you at a later time." He will probably keep sticking the microphone in your face in hopes of vexing you into an outburst or a flight, but resist the urge to shout or flee. It's unlikely he'll ever use on the air your calm invitation to a sit-down interview because it would raise the question in the viewer's mind of why he didn't take you up on that invitation.

Understand that an ambush TV interview is more a theatrical, than a journalistic, tactic, and in the event you find yourself in this situation, play the role of the sober, reasoned, cooperative but, alas, unavailable statesman. More often than not, doing that takes all the drama from this particular aspect of the reporter's story. For example, had Dan Rather said to Steve Wilson: "I'm sorry, Steve, but I'm late for an interview of my own and I have to leave now, but I'll be happy to talk with you at a later time and date. Just call my office and make an appointment," No one would have run a clip of him saying that. In fact, Rather had an even better calm and rational way out of the ambush. Wilson's story *did* involve an active legal case, and CBS corporate policy prohibited discussing current or pending litigation. But instead of using that completely legitimate excuse for not speaking to Wilson, Rather embarrassed himself and gave Wilson and "Entertainment Tonight" a great story.

If a camera appears out of nowhere and it's accompanied by an aggressive reporter shouting questions, it's an ambush and you gain nothing by stopping and accommodating him.

How to Win a Shoutfest

An ambush, offers no door to your agenda, but a broadcast shoutfest, despite daunting challenges, will afford you an opportunity to shoehorn in some of your messages. A shoutfest is one of those television news interview programs that feature bitterly partisan and emotionally hectoring "experts" and "analysts" engaging in furious yelling matches. Often there is so much overtalking the listener hears nothing but an angry babble. For reasons unfathomable to me, audiences must be responding to this heat-instead-of-light approach because there are quite a few of these exercises in sound and fury. Serious journalistic efforts like PBS's "The News Hour" and "Charlie Rose" don't tolerate these bullying encounters, but those sober discussions are becoming the exception and not the rule in broadcast panel shows.

In general, the shoutfests deal with political and social matters. If you are the spokesperson for a political, social, or even an economic issue that might spark controversy, you may be invited on such a program. If, on the other hand, you are the spokesperson for a new product or service or for a scientific breakthrough, it's less likely you'll be asked to appear in one of these raucous encounters. (As I noted earlier, climate scientists may find themselves an exception. Despite the fact that as of this writing 97.3 percent of all climate change studies indicate the climate is warming and human activity is a major factor in that change, broadcasters, seeking Fear and Fury, often "balance" the story by granting false equivalency — equal time and weight — to deniers).

If you're scheduled to appear on a shoutfest, watch the show so you can identify the style and agenda of the host. Many hosts of these shows have an ideological bias, and you should know if that bias favors your angels or your devils. Watching will also give you insights into how far he'll let the talkover go before intervening.

Preparation, as always, is key to mastery, however in a shoutfest you need to abandon reasoned argument and become a sloganeer. Prepare your slogans by reducing your agenda points to their barest essentials, to verbal headlines. When you're on the air, shout them unabashedly into the fray whenever you can. In this effort you'll find an ally in human biology, because often your best opportunity to shoehorn in a point is when an opponent takes a breath. Fortunately, even the most long-winded panelist must draw in air to propel his rants.

In a shoutfest, toss out all rules of etiquette. You don't need to be responding to a question and there need be no context to your message points; just ram them in. Most of what the audience hears is babble, so if you can launch a PMS in the clear, listeners are going to assume it had a context. It's possible that your interjection may lead the moderator to follow up with a direct question or, at least, steer the discussion to your point. Conversely, it's important for you not to get drawn too deeply into your opponent's tirade, lest you wind up just shouting responses no one is going to hear anyway. You really don't want to address his points or, at least, you don't want to answer them in any detail, because if you do, you're serving his agenda.

None of this makes any conversational sense, but watch the shows — what about them does make sense? Some feature three, four, or five people trying to out-yell each other, often all of them speaking at the same time — if speaking isn't too generous a word for it. Complex issues are reduced to angry slogans. If you can deliver the few seconds of light amid the many minutes of heat, you've gone a long way toward winning. One added thought: don't be shy. If you've ever watched a show with three or more panel members — such as Bill Maher's "Real Time" on HBO — you've probably noticed in almost every edition, one of the panelists plays the role of shrinking violet, getting only a tiny fraction of the airtime grabbed aggressively by the others. On these programs, if you are shy, retiring, reticent — even polite — you're going to be that shortchanged panelist. It may go against your personal grain, but you've got to jump in with both feet and swing away. Let the other panelists fend for themselves; your concern is your agenda and expressing it, nothing more.

More civil than shoutfests — and far more conducive to calm, rational, and even *thorough* expression of ideas — are print and online interviews. I'll deal with those in the next chapter.

TAKING NOTES:
PRINT & EMAIL INTERVIEWS

The oldest and the newest of the media share more simi-larities than differences. Stories in newspapers, magazines, and in online news outlets are often the work of a single reporter, as opposed to the work of a team (as in TV), and print and online outlets are generally able to devote more space to a story than broadcasters. Print and online media are better venues for ana-lytical journalism and for stories requiring detailed, intricate, and complex data. Since print has been around longer, let's begin with that venerable medium.

PRINT INTERVIEWS
Print was the first mass medium and to this day is general-ly the most thorough of all the various forms of media. Movable type, perfected by Jonhannes Gutenberg in the 15th century, en-abled printers to report and disseminate news within just a few days or even hours after they learned of it. Since printing elimi-nated the arduous labor of hand-copying all documents, written material became less expensive and literacy exploded — reading was no longer the exclusive province of the clergy, the nobility, and the very wealthy. As literacy spread, newspapers were born and in just a few short centuries their circulation expanded geo-metrically, reaching impressive levels in America during the ear-ly 20th century. In those times, competition for audiences and for advertising dollars was, for the most part, among the print outlets, not between them and other media. In cities such as New York, there were more than a dozen daily English-language newspapers as well as dailies printed in Chinese, Greek, German, Italian, Russian, Polish, and Yiddish. Adding the weekly com-munity and ethnic newspapers brought the total of newsy jour-nals in that city alone to more than 100! Even back in 1961, when I graduated from Columbia University's School of Journal-ism, there remained four citywide mass-circulation morning dai-ly newspapers and three afternoon dailies. Today there are just three citywide dailies. That total, however is two more than

most American cities have. In a few cities, the remaining daily is no longer available in printed form every day. The Pulitzer prize-winning New Orleans Times-Picayune went from being a printed daily to being a thrice-weekly printed newspaper, keeping a seven-day-a-week schedule only online.

The most precious commodity of the broadcast media is time; the equivalent commodity in print journalism is space. On a big news day, a paper can add space by adding pages. It can get bigger or smaller as dictated by the space needs of either the day's news or advertising or both. An hour of broadcast time is fixed by the speed of the earth's rotation and so it is an absolute: sixty minutes. An hour cannot be expanded to sixty-two minutes to accommodate a big story. And, in fact, a commercial broadcast hour is really closer to forty-four minutes once you subtract the commercials. If you're thinking that's skimpy, consider that the ratio of editorial content to advertising is four-to-one in broadcasting but more like one-to-one in print. In fact, some newspapers print more advertising than news, especially in their Sunday editions, while no news program runs more minutes of commercials than minutes of news content. Another difference: publications have the reread factor — if you don't understand a sentence, or can't identify a spokesperson, you can slow down and analyze the sentence or search earlier in the story for the spokesperson's affiliation. But broadcast journalism doesn't have that luxury: you get it first time or you miss it. In fact, when you are the reader, you can study a complex story slowly or zip through a simple one quickly. In TV and radio, the pace of the story is completely out of your hands. A corollary to the reread factor in print journalism is the disregard factor. You can toss out those advertising supplements on Sunday, skip the display ads, and just concentrate on the news stories. There are ways to skip the advertising in a linear medium like television: you can use the commercial breaks to go to the refrigerator or to the bathroom, or you can buy and use a digital video recording device like TiVo, which can fast-forward through commercials. But for many TV viewers and for all radio listeners, random access to information is not an option. Print media usually offer a table of contents or a news index, so you can turn directly to the information you want. In broadcasting there is no such convenience.

Despite the greater news-to-advertising ratio in broadcasting, on a routine basis the print media allot far more space to news than broadcast media allot time. When I worked on newspapers, all the space devoted to material other than advertising and regular features like stock tables and comic strips was called, rather inelegantly, the news hole. In the middle of the 20th century, when there were so many newspapers looking for material to fill their news holes, legions of print reporters worked the streets and phones to develop stories. The ranks of publications, especially dailies, has thinned, and uncompromising economic dictates have resulted in firing sweeps through the editorial offices of the surviving journals. The legions of print reporters have been reduced to mere squads. My local newspaper, *The Los Angeles Times*, hard on the heels of winning a batch of Pulitzer prizes, announced yet another round of editorial staff cuts mandated by its Chicago-based parent company. This, unfortunately, is not unusual. In 2007, the *Philadelphia Inquirer* pink-slipped 68 of its 412 editorial employees and Time, Inc. cut loose 172 of its editors, reporters, and writers. These substantial cuts were part of a national trend which, in 2006 alone, saw *17,809* media jobs eliminated. In fact the Pew Research Center reports that between 2000 and 2012 there was a 32 percent reduction in the number of newspaper editorial employees and a 43 percent reduction in the number of newspaper photographers. Even though editorial ranks may be thinning and the number of newspapers continues to spiral downward, print remains the medium where your message is likely to get its most thorough examination. So it's important to consider how you best communicate to readers through the remaining inky wretches who practice the ancient craft of print journalism.

THE GRAMMATICAL IMPERATIVE

Back in the 1960s when I was a reporter for the now-defunct *New York World-Telegram and The Sun*, the city's chief executive was the three-term mayor, Robert F. Wagner, Jr. Mayor Wagner routinely butchered English syntax when he spoke. In fact, he often tortured grammar until it screamed for mercy. And mercy is what grammar got from the print reporters covering him because just as routinely as Wagner tore sentences apart, we reporters put them back together for him. Back then, reporters were in the habit of doing the mayor — and other interview subjects — the favor of "fixing their quotes." We did not change the meaning of what they said, we just improved their grammar and syntax; repair work we performed with barely a second thought.

Today reporters and editors no longer fix an interview subject's tortured phrases. The party responsible for this is the same beast that slew all those New York newspapers: television. As my print colleagues and I saw fewer of our number and more TV crews at news conferences, we also saw the light of truth — or the light of the dead-on accurate quote. I couldn't very well fix Mayor Wagner's quote in the *World-Telegram* if my reader was going to put down the paper, turn on the television, and see the butchered original for himself.

The wording of your quotes in print interviews is exclusively in your hands, so make every effort to speak clearly, grammatically, and in complete sentences. The biggest fix a contemporary reporter might make is to add in brackets words you've omitted in an answer.

It's more important to speak grammatically and in complete sentences for print media than it is for broadcast. Broadcasters are not as likely to toss out a grammatically sloppy soundbite as are print reporters. There are two reasons for this. First, broadcasting needs soundbites, even if they are imperfect. If a broadcast reporter paraphrases everything an interview subject says, the story will look and sound boring; it will be a reportorial monologue. So broadcast journalists will cut you more slack and use an grammatical soundbite just for the sake of getting another voice in the story. Second, broadcasting is just not as discriminating about proper English. Half a century ago, John Hohenberg, one of my professors at Columbia's School of Journalism, railed, "Broadcast copy is bad copy." If you listen carefully to what's said and read on radio and television today, you'll agree. A good deal of what broadcast reporters say is grammatically incorrect. This is true not only when they are speaking off-the-cuff, but also when they are working from a prompter or script. They write the stuff ungrammatically! If you had the opportunity to read most radio and television news scripts, you would find they are rife with incomplete sentences and bad syntax. "More than" routinely becomes "over" in broadcast scripts, as in, "He worked for the city for over thirty years." On television, things are "real good," as opposed to the correct "really good." The difference between "lie" and "lay" seems beyond the ken of most broadcasters. Also, very few *literally* know the difference between "literally" and "figuratively." Why are radio and television news scripts so cavalier about language? Because, broadcasters claim, they are writing for the ear and not the eye.

So in the grammatical skid row of broadcasting, your ragged, sloppy soundbite doesn't particularly stand out. On the other hand, readers of newspapers and magazines see your syntactical-ly-challenged quote surrounded by prose written and edited in conformity to the rules of grammar. Because of this, a print re-porter is less likely than a broadcaster to use a really badly con-structed direct quote, preferring instead to paraphrase you. Do yourself and the print reporter the favor of giving him quotes he can use, not quotes he'll have to paraphrase. And, by the way, it doesn't hurt to speak grammatically on radio and TV.

SUBJECTIVITY AND OBJECTIVITY

Print is at once the most subjective and objective medium. Let's deal with objectivity first. I noted earlier that print media devote many more column inches to stories than broadcast de-votes time to the same story. The exception, of course, is satura-tion coverage — the sort of broadcasting we saw on 9/11, after the space shuttle Columbia disaster, and in the extensive cover-age of hurricanes Katrina and Sandy. Broadcasters call this sort of reporting "wall-to-wall" coverage. Wall-to-wall coverage aside, if you were to read aloud a newspaper account of most stories, it would far eclipse the account of the same event in a typical newscast. For example, I read aloud an article in a recent *Los Angeles Times* about shelters in St. Louis that were over-whelmed by a flood of newly homeless persons. The exercise took me seven minutes. That's nearly a third of the twenty-two minutes of editorial content in a half-hour newscast. Similarly, if you set in type even a substantial television news story and printed it in newspaper column form, its brevity would be star-tling — no TV news story would run more than six or seven column inches. This difference accounts for the greater amount of both objectivity and subjectivity in the print media.

The relative abundance of space that a newspaper or mag-azine can devote to a story enables objectivity; there is space in a print story for all sides to be expressed and for those expressions to run long enough to be thorough explanations. If you are a spokesperson for one of those sides, the effectiveness of your advocacy is up to you. If you give good quotes, they'll be used, and if you don't, you'll be paraphrased. If you can make your Positive Message Statements relevant and telling, they'll be in the story. If you can be specific, there's room to include the specifics you cite. In the homeless shelter story, for instance, the reporter detailed four case histories, including one of a single mother who moved into a homeless shelter because, although she had a full-time job, her rent ate up more than half her income. Ironically, that job was social services counselor. In other words, she helped needy families find resources, including housing. That specific made the story dramatic and vivid. Had a local commercial television station done that same story, it would have run 90 seconds to two minutes and likely would have told only that ironic story of the homeless social worker.

In a story with several contending points of view, print is apt to give more space to the debate. If equal treatment of your idea and an opposing idea fill six column inches of newspaper space, the equivalent amount of broadcast time simply wouldn't be available in a daily newscast. Additionally, because television is so dependent on images and both radio and television are so dependent on soundbites, they are less likely to run subjective opinion or analytical pieces. Usually, the pictures and soundbites are wanting in these stories, so they don't make very compelling viewing or listening; subjective and analytical journalism is pretty much the province of the print media. A major exception: anchors on some cable news channels have license to exhibit subjectivity and they increasingly express their opinions at the expense, in airtime, of factual reporting.

In the fall of 2002, Senate Majority Leader Trent Lott made a feeble joke during the celebration of Senator Strom Thurmond's 100th birthday. Noting Thurmond's Dixiecrat run for the presidency in 1948, Lott said that had Thurmond, an outspoken segregationist, won "we wouldn't have had all these problems over all these years." The media coverage of this bit of career self-destruction is instructive. White House spokespersons were willing to talk, but not on camera, not on the record, and not for direct attribution. So the news stories were analytical. What did we see on the nightly newscasts? Each network's White House correspondent stood on the lawn in front of the executive mansion telling us — without benefit of pictures or soundbites — what the thinking was inside the building visible over his shoulder. The lack of pictures and soundbites dictated that the stories be short. Had you set them in type and laid them into a newspaper column, they would have run only two or three inches. Compare that with the feet and yards, perhaps miles, of column space that print reporters produced on the same story, also working without those direct quotes. This was a dramatic demonstration that newspaper and magazine writers are less reliant on direct quotes to tell a story, so it's key that you make your points compellingly quoteworthy when you are dealing with the print media.

Also, it's important to determine the purpose of a print reporter's interview. Is she seeking background for a think piece or is the interview destined for inclusion in a news story? If it's the think piece, your direct quotes will likely count for less — they may never see the light of day, although the columnist may paraphrase your ideas. If the interview is for a news story, your quotes count for more; they are the only way for you to be directly represented in the story. While you're less likely to be directly quoted in the think piece, you can use a background interview to further your agenda even though your exact words won't appear. But if you think you're giving a columnist information on a not-for-attribution basis, think again. As I wrote earlier, these days it's hard for a reporter to maintain confidentiality. Therefore, I recommend only saying on a not-for-attribution basis what you would ordinarily say *for* attribution.

Going back to the Trent Lott story, it was easy to ascertain then-President George W. Bush's attitude about the majority leader's ouster although the President made exactly one public statement of rebuke and, in that statement, did not call for Lott to step down from the leadership. Anyone who read a newspaper knew that President Bush wanted Lott out. Analysts kept writing of the *White House*'s displeasure with Lott and the *White House*'s desire that he step down. To read it literally, the building itself, rather than its principal occupant, had an opinion. The opinion expressed was, of course, the president's and the information came in not-for-attribution discussions.

Before sitting down for an interview with a print reporter, it's a good idea to marshal on paper as many facts as you can, and to let the reporter have them to take away with her. Photographs and other visual aides help, too. Even if the newspaper doesn't run the photograph, a picture may enable the reporter to more accurately describe what you're talking about. If you are dealing with a new product, have a sample standing by and let the reporter use it. Sometimes this will yield a good third-party recommendation, as in: "This reporter tried the new MP3 player and found the audio reproduction to be the equal of the CD player in a high-end stereo system." *Never* offer the reporter a free product; he might construe that as a bribe and report it as such. Reputable newspapers and magazines may buy or borrow a product for testing, but will not accept a freebee. Although there are unethical reporters who are "on the take," it is dangerous to assume you're dealing with one. In fact, even if a reporter solicits a gift, you should refuse. Any reporter who does that should be turned in to his employer immediately. And if you've followed my advice and recorded your sessions with reporters, you've got proof of his unethical venality.

HOW NOT TO DO A PRINT INTERVIEW

Discussing the importance of not copping an attitude in Chapter 3, I mentioned a 2003 interview Martha Stewart gave *The New Yorker*. The interview was in connection with the insider trading accusations against her for her sale of ImClone stock in December, 2002. Let's look at that interview again because it is a textbook case of how not to do a print interview.

First, some background: Ms. Stewart sold her 40,000 shares of ImClone stock for $228,000 in December, 2002, one day after ImClone's chief executive, Sam Waksal, learned the Food and Drug Administration was not going to approve a drug the company had developed. Waksal, who immediately began unloading his shares of ImClone, spoke with Martha Stewart, an investor and longtime friend. After that conversation, Ms. Stewart sold her ImClone shares. For his part, Waksal agreed to plead guilty to insider trading, so much could be made — and was made — by the media of the Waksal-Stewart phone call that preceded Ms. Stewart's stock sale.

The Waksal-Stewart conversation and Ms. Stewart's sale of stock came immediately after Christmas, 2002, the conversation on December 26, the stock sale on December 27. The controversy erupted almost immediately. But Ms. Stewart did not speak to *The New Yorker*'s legal correspondent, Jeffrey Toobin, until sometime in mid to late January. Toobin's article appeared in the magazine's February 3 edition — more than a month after the controversial stock trade. In the weeks between the trade and the publication of the article, the media were free to speculate about the case with no input whatsoever from Martha Stewart — and speculate they did. That speculation did great damage to Ms. Stewart's cause and to her finances. In *The New Yorker* article, Ms. Stewart said that the cost to her personally from lost business, depressed value of her company's shares, and legal fees totaled $400 million.

So her delay — not getting out in front of the story early on — was a mistake. It looked as if Martha Stewart had been indifferent to public opinion and felt no need to address the charges in the media, whereas her accusers, the federal prosecution team, were not at all reluctant to go public. Ms. Stewart did have one previous brief brush with a reporter; she was questioned about the case by CBS News correspondent Jill Clayson during one of the domestic diva's regularly scheduled live appearances on the CBS "Early Show." This happened immediately after the charges surfaced, and Ms. Stewart responded to Ms. Clayson by saying that everything would turn out all right and she wasn't there to discuss the charges but to do a cooking segment. Chef's knife in hand and looking annoyed, Ms. Stewart continued chopping a cabbage with determined vigor. Those who saw the episode likely felt that she was ducking the issue, and — perhaps — imagining that the cabbage was the impertinent Ms. Clayson. The cooking segment became fodder for late night comedians and CBS discontinued Ms. Stewart's appearances on "The Early Show" after that.

A good rule for stories likely to become controversial is to get out in front of them, not to wait around until a reporter asks you to react. This is true even if you are able to say very little. A more media-savvy move for Ms. Stewart might have been to take advantage of the CBS appearance and indicate that she was donating the profits from the stock sale to charity. The cost of the donation would have been minuscule compared to the financial damage Ms. Stewart reported to Toobin. Also, if there were shades of gray in the case, authorities might have cut some slack to a public figure who had donated to charity any profits from her alleged wrongdoing. The media, certainly, would have been much harder-pressed to crusade against a caring and open Martha Stewart than against a seemingly evasive and indifferent one.

Ms. Stewart's second mistake in her *New Yorker* interview: she went off the record. It is clear from even a casual reading of Toobin's article that she is the source of some of the unattributed assertions that buttress her side of the argument. Toobin writes at the beginning of his piece that Ms. Stewart agreed to talk with him about her feelings, but that she declined to discuss the facts of the case *on the record* — an indication that she discussed those facts off the record.

Her third mistake was to have her agenda right there in front of her where her interviewer could see it. Toobin reports that she had a pad in front of her with points she wanted to get into the interview. Having your notes in front of you invites the journalist to tell his readers just that — that you had your notes in front of you. Surely Ms. Stewart, an accomplished and extraordinarily bright woman, could have memorized her message points.

Ms. Stewart's fourth mistake was inviting Toobin to do the interview in her home, a restored early 19th Century farmhouse. That was probably a calculated risk, but it did not pay off because part of the piece was a house tour and animal census and neither furthered Ms. Stewart's cause. Toobin straightforwardly reported the astounding attention to detail at Ms. Stewart's house. Among items he described were custom-tailored fabric frost covers cut to the individual shape of each outdoor shrub. Toobin mentions them without sarcasm; readers certainly can supply that reaction without prompting by the writer. As to the animal census, Toobin describes a house which sounds like a menagerie for domesticated animals. According to the article, there were two dogs, five cats and thirty singing canaries — but only because it was canary mating season. The house itself "reads" like some sort of stage set, with Ms. Stewart attended by a substantial staff of spin doctors and domestic help. This distanced Ms. Stewart from the public she was trying to court.

The title of Toobin's piece is "Lunch at Martha's," although the interview began before lunch, ran through the meal, and extended beyond it. As indicated in Chapter 4, a meal is a meal and an interview is an interview, and it's a bad idea to mix the two. The normal pitfalls of a mealtime interview — interruptions by servers and the distraction of food — were exacerbated when Ms. Stewart spontaneously gave Toobin the recipe for one of the many Chinese dishes they were having and insisted he write it down. At that point, without Toobin's adding any nuance to his account, Ms. Stewart descended into self-parody.

Another hideous moment for Ms. Stewart's cause arose when she pointed out to Toobin that in ancient Chinese society the higher one's social class, the thinner one's chopsticks were. She then announced that she sought out and bought the thinnest chopsticks she could find. She added: "Maybe that's why people hate me." That was too good a quote for Toobin to skip.

Ms. Stewart's thin chopstick sensibility pervades the tone of Toobin's piece.* Her attitude was so manifestly self-absorbed and so indifferent to the public that she emerged looking worse than if she had not done the interview at all. She certainly failed in her attempt to rally public sympathy for her plight. Interestingly, Martha Stewart's next interview — a television session with Barbara Walters — was as good as her print interview was bad. But by the time she granted the Walters interview, the damage was done. In fact, Walters interviewed Stewart on the eve of her brief stint in federal prison. (In an ironic postscript, in 2009 the FDA approved the drug, Cetuximab.)

TELEPHONE INTERVIEWS

Toobin's interview with Martha Stewart was a face-to-face encounter, but more often than not newspaper, magazine and even radio interviews are conducted over the phone. In a phone encounter you have no visual clues to your interviewer's attitude, expression, or demeanor. Still, phone interviews offer some unique advantages over in-person interviews. Those advantages come with a downside, too.

For the media, the advantages of phoners are obvious: a print or radio reporter sitting at his desk and working the phones can reach many contacts in the time it might take him to travel to one venue and interview a single source. Additionally, the phoner gives the reporter the flexibility to call you, interview you, call someone else, get a different point of view on the subject, and call you back to get your reaction — setting the stage for a good, conflict of quotes in his story Even "beat" reporters use the phone extensively. A reporter assigned to Congress is more likely to phone various congressional sources for quotes and information than he is to wander the halls of the institution, knocking on doors to see sources in person.

I estimate that 80 to 90 percent of the interviews I conducted during my newspaper career were phoners. I wrote hundreds of stories without ever seeing the interview subjects. I had a fair number of regular sources and contact whom I never met in person; they were solely telephone sources.

---

* You can read the Toobin piece online. Google, "The New Yorker, Lunch at Martha's," and you'll find a link to it.

A phone call from a reporter will not necessarily come to your office during normal business hours. A reporter might call you at home and at odd hours. Most morning newspapers lock their first editions sometime between 9 and 11 p.m. Reporters seeking information on stories may work the phones right up until that deadline. So if you're a source, don't be surprised to pick up a late evening phone call and find a journalist on the line. Calling people at 9 p.m. or later seeking a comment on a story often yields far more unguarded statements than calls made during business hours.

Even television, that most visual of media, will sometimes uses phone interviews when there are no other options. Usually this involves a breaking story and an interview subject who is at a location inaccessible to cameras. The day Islamic extremists assassinated Egyptian President Anwar Sadat, I made a decision to keep "Good Morning America" on the air beyond its normal two hours and we filled the earliest part of the third hour by interviewing prominent commentators and experts over the phone until we could get live guests into our New York and Washington studios. By remaining on the air using phoners, we were in position to be the first network program to report that Sadat was dead and not, as Egyptian spokespersons initially reported, merely wounded. Today a producer would likely try to set up a Skype interview first and resort to an ordinary phone call as a last resort. (Skype interview details are in the next chapter.)

THE UP- AND DOWNSIDES OF PHONERS

The advantages of phone interviews for the reporter are obvious. And there are advantages for you as well, but there is also a downside. Let's deal with the negative first. Think about how we normally converse on the phone. Without eye contact, we tend to be more open, more confidential, and more revealing of our feelings than we are in face-to-face conversations. Unable to see the response of the other party, we imagine his acceptance of our argument and his agreement with our points — why else does he stay on the line? That assumed agreement leads to still more openness on our part. That openness is a pitfall in phone interviews with the media. You are talking to a reporter using the same instrument that leads you into natural, relaxed conversation with your best friend, but a reporter is never your best friend. The telephone has a way of lulling you into a state of self-revelation that may lead you to stray from your agenda, casually stroll up the gallows steps, and hang yourself with your own words.

Be on guard when doing media phoners. When you talk to a reporter on the phone, you are working, not chatting. No matter how conversational the reporter gets, she is working, too. In fact, that casual, conversational attitude she strikes on the phone is most likely just a highly refined technique she uses to get sources to be more revelatory than they really want to be. The pitfall of phoners is more than overcome by the big advantage: a telephone interview is an open-book test.

Have your Positive Message Statements laid out on a table or desk in front of you. If you've noticed that there is a flaw in your interview technique, you can post notes to yourself such as "Slow Down!" or "Give Specifics!" or "Remember Why Should I Care!" Having these cues at hand will remind you of two things: First, you are not having a casual chat, but are working; and, second, that the goal of your work is getting your agenda through the reporter to her readers or listeners. You are not cheating on your college geology test if you read your agenda points during a phoner. They are not crib notes; they are your points. The reporter may well be reading her questions, so why not read your answers? As a practical technique for taking this open book test, I recommend writing each message point on a separate index card and spreading the cards out on your desk. When you work one into the interview, turn the card over — that way you are less likely to repeat any of your agenda points unnecessarily and you'll have a clear indication of your remaining points. When you are looking at the backs of all your cards, turn them over and revisit them. You want to stay on-message throughout the interview.

To guard against becoming too chatty during phone interviews, I encourage clients to stand up and gesture broadly. If you do that, you won't fall into the trap of putting your feet up on the desk, letting down your guard, and saying something you will later regret. Also, expansive gestures help make your voice more interesting for radio interviews conducted over the phone.

CALLS OUT OF THE BLUE

If a reporter phones you out of the blue and he wants to do an interview right then and there, say "No." These calls are the equivalent of a TV ambush interview. You need to buy yourself enough time to get organized, to create an agenda, to figure out who your audience is, and to check online to see what's going on in your world. You also need time to find out if the reporter is, in fact, who he claims to be and if the story he's working on is the story he described to you or if that is a just a cover to engage you in a conversation about something else. In fact, the "reporter" on the phone may not be a reporter at all — something you'll learn by calling him back at his publication or radio station. A fake reporter could be a competitor on a fishing expedition or someone with an ax to grind. I heard of one possibly apocryphal case where a private detective, identifying himself as a reporter, called someone in an attempt to lure him into making slanderous remarks against a particularly litigious client who was looking for grounds to file a lawsuit.

When you get a call without warning, you are well within your rights to suggest a later time for the interview. Tell the reporter, "I can't talk to you right now, Let me call you back in two hours." If he says he's on deadline, be suspicious. Oftentimes he's not on deadline at all, but says he is because he fears you won't call back. Sometimes his deadline is self-imposed or even a fiction; he wants to complete his interview with you so he can call a second source and get reaction to your comments. Or, he wants to get this out of the way and move on to another story. Reporters don't like to wait until they are on deadline to write stories; in the rush they may do sloppy work, so take the "I'm on deadline" with more than a grain of salt. Early in my career, when I began working as a reporter for *The New York World-Telegram and Sun,* I sat next to a veteran newsman who was *always* on deadline. It was funny to hear him tell someone at 10 a.m. that he was on deadline and then hear him tell another source he was on deadline at 4 p.m. The real deadline for the section of the paper we worked on was 6 p.m. Nonetheless, his ploy of "I'm on deadline" almost always worked.

If the reporter phoning you really is on deadline, he may have waited until the last minute for a reason — specifically so you don't have time to prepare an adequate response. This was a trick Bob Woodward and Carl Bernstein of the *Washington Post* often used during their Watergate investigation, and they chronicled that practice in their book *All the President's Men.* As an example, they would call Attorney General John Mitchell just before deadline so that there was no time for his team to concoct a response or to do damage control. I am not saying all reporters calling on deadline are trying to entrap you. When news

144

breaks right up against a deadline a reporter is trying to get comments on the fast moving developments and there is no trickery involved. You will know those instances by the circumstances of the story. If your plant sprang a leak of toxic chemicals half an hour before the local newspaper's deadline, the reporter is not playing games when he calls you and says he's on deadline. Still, never talk to a cold caller right away; call him back — even if your delay is only five or ten minutes. You need time to organize yourself and your ideas for the interview.

Those deadline calls will frequently come to your home, even if you have an unlisted number. Reporters are adept at ferreting out unlisted numbers, cell phone numbers, and home e-mail accounts.

If your company or organization has a public relations or public affairs department or outside public relations counsel, call a representative before returning a reporter's cold call. The public relations professional may have insights into the reporter's story as well as recommendations for your agenda. If the story involves a controversy, you want to be sure that you are on the same page as the rest of your organization when you speak with the reporter.

Once you've made satisfactory arrangements for the interview, array your PMSs in front of you, round up any additional notes you may need, and — as a guard against misstatements — invite in a witness to hear your side of the interview. Then set up your recorder. Most phones can be hooked into a simple, inexpensive device that permits recording of both sides of a conversation. (I bought one at Radio Shack for under $50.) Additionally, many home answering machines can record both sides of a phone call as can most smartphones.

When you are set up, call the reporter, alert him that you are recording the interview, and tell him how much time you can devote to him ("I can give you ten minutes — I'm sure that will be adequate.") If the interview is going very well, you can extend the ten minutes to 12 or 15, or even 20 minutes. If you're dissatisfied with the interview's progress, stick to the time limit you announced at the outset. Put a timer to the conversation so you know exactly when you can bail out if it is going poorly. With each question the reporter asks, study your index cards and see whether the question leads logically to one of your agenda points or whether there is a relatively easy bridge you can build to one of your PMSs. Don't be shy about reading your PMSs.

He can't see you and it's the best way of getting them into the interview. After you deploy each PMS, turn your index card over. When you've worked them all into the interview, turn them face up again and revisit them; stay on-message!

Take your time before answering questions. There is no law that says you must begin talking as soon as a reporter ends her question. If you want to buy time, say something like, "Let me think of the best way to answer that" or "There are several ways to answer that, let me figure out which one will be easiest for your readers to understand."

My most successful interview was a phoner with *TV Guide.* I did not just have a list of Positive Message Statements; I had quips, jokes, pithy comments — all of which I had written in advance. When I was executive producer of "Good Morning America," show business reporter Rona Barrett was lured away by the "Today Show," and as a replacement we hired and then quickly fired a woman I'll call Mary Sunshine. Mary did the best audition I'd ever seen and followed it with thirteen weeks of disappointing performance. Mary got distracted by the perks of her job and spent too much of her time and energy on them and not enough on gathering gossipy show business news for her daily segment. One glaring example: she spent two-thirds of her very generous wardrobe allowance on shoes, although on-air she always appeared seated behind a desk talking directly to camera. In 13 weeks, viewers never once saw her feet and those pricey shoes.

When ABC fired Mary, she did not go quietly into the night but called *TV Guide* with her version of her abbreviated career. The magazine saw a good conflict and hence a good story — little David (Mary) versus big, bad Goliath (ABC). As the show's executive producer, I was Goliath's spokesperson — if not Goliath himself. I knew *TV Guide* would go into this story with a pro-David attitude. How could they not? So I had my work cut out for me. Aware it was going to be an uphill battle, I sat down at my typewriter — which tells what ancient history this story is — and wrote out every point I thought Mary might make in her interview. I then wrote responses to every one of them, making those responses as quoteworthy as I could.

The *TV Guide* writer was in California, where Mary Sunshine lived, and I was in New York, so my interview was a phoner. I had my tape recorder hooked up and my index cards arrayed on my desk in front of me. As the interview progressed, the reporter's questions indicated that I had anticipated all Mary's complaints. For each question that came out of those complaints I had not just an answer, but a concise, pithy quote. When I was preparing for the interview, I came up with one line that really pleased me and I thought, "This one ought to be the last line of the article." When the article appeared, it *was* the last line. After describing the shoe travesty, I said to the *TV Guide* reporter: "The problem with Mary Sunshine was she fell in love with her limousine and forgot where it was going." The quote not only ended the article, but also epitomized its tone. On that rare occasion, Goliath won.

I tell you this story not to pat my own back for being clever, but to show just how effective you can be by having message points prepared in advance and by using them during a phone interview. Remember, your preparation is only half the assignment. Your notes are there to be used. On a number of occasions in media training sessions, I've had clients go through the exercise of preparing messages for phone interviews only to leave them sitting on the desk in front of them, unread and unused. When I see them doing that I throw this question into the interview, "Aren't you going to use those great notes you've prepared?" That usually gets a laugh, but it also produces the desired reaction: they begin using their notes. For reasons unclear to me, some people are uncomfortable reading — or even referring to — written material during an interview. Get over it! Take advantage of the unique opportunity you have in a phoner; use your notes to get all your points across. All the preinterview preparation in the world is of no use if you don't use what you've prepared. As with an open book test, the opportunity is lost if you don't bring the book, open it and use it for every answer.

GETTING AN ADVANCE LOOK AT A STORY

Most publications and broadcast outlets forbid reporters and producers from showing a story to a source in advance. In fact, if you request an advance copy of a story you will likely get a firm "no," and you may turn the reporter against you.

But there is one way to get some advance knowledge that is not off-putting to a journalist: offer to fact-check. If I were to say, "Of course, you'll be sending me your story in advance so I can change and correct it," I would get that firm "no." But if I were to say, "If you'd like to fact check anything I've given you in this interview, feel free to email it to me," I may well get not just my quotes and assertions but also — on occasion — the full story.

Not every reporter will send you her full story when you offer to fact-check, but if she does send you your quotes and any assertions of fact you have made, you've got an opportunity to correct errors and to suggest stronger language to buttress your agenda points.

Even if a reporter declines your offer to fact-check, you have another fallback, another turn at bat, in effect. If you've followed my advice and recorded the interview, play it back as soon as you get off the phone or as soon as the reporter leaves your office. If you misspoke or can do better with some of your soundbites, call the reporter and say something like, "I just came up with a better way of saying...." Most reporters hearing "better way" — or the even more-compelling "more accurate way...." — will be happy to change your quote or add your information. Remember, a story is a work in progress until it's published or broadcast. A reporter will not hesitate to call you back and ask a question she neglected to ask during your interview. Don't hesitate to call her if you made a mistake, omitted an agenda point, or come up with a better grabber.

Some of the more thorough publications, like *The New Yorker*, maintain a separate fact-checking department to vet every assertion of fact. However newspapers — with their tighter deadlines and scores of stories in each edition — do not fact-check that way. A thorough, ethical reporter may well take advantage of your offer to fact-check her story, especially if there are technical, scientific, medical, or other arcane details in it.

EMAIL INTERVIEWS

Over the last decade or so, journalists have become increasingly willing to accept an email exchange of questions and answers. This is especially true for reporters working for online journals like *The Huffington Post* and *Politico.com*. The reporter submits a list of questions to an interview subject via email. The subject emails back her answers and if the reporter has follow-ups, he emails these, too. The advantage to you, the spokesperson, is obvious. Composing your answers off-line and then emailing them to the reporter gives you total control, insuring that you can work in all your message points and that you can make your responses quoteworthy. Most journalists prefer the give-and-take of a live interview conducted either in person or over the phone, because their follow-ups are organic to your responses. But with pressure to be productive (i.e. report and write more stories in less time using fewer resources) today's reporters often don't have a choice and must go with email exchanges. In the finished story the reporter may stipulate your answers were emailed responses to emailed questions. But so what? If your quotes are used and they are effective, your agenda has been served. Today's readers don't care that the interview was conducted via email.

The biggest advantage of an email interview is the time you buy for researching and honing your answers. Just be sure you take full advantage of the opportunity by carefully parsing your answers, printing them out, and reading them before launching them into the cyberspace by hitting that email "send" button.

The online versions of conventional media — especially newspapers — are growing more important. Mobile apps bring newspaper and magazine journalism to smartphones and tablets as well as to computer screens. The web edition staffs of some newspapers are large — more than 100 of the *New York Times'* newsroom employees do more work on the web edition than on the print version of the paper. Most print reporters file stories online first and continually update them before they appear in print. Many reporters are also writing blogs — often containing more detailed information and more behind-the-story insights. At the same time as print newspaper circulation has been dropping, journals' Internet readership has been growing. The web and mobile apps are attractive to cash-squeezed print journalism because the production costs are half those of the paper editions. ("No trucks, no trees," is how the Boston Globe's publisher described the cost benefit.) As this trend grows, we are sure to see further dependence on email question-and-answer exchanges. An advantage to a news source is that an error in the online version of a story can be corrected quickly and likely will be seen by far fewer people than a similar error in the print version of the newspaper.

Whether you are interviewed for a cyber journal or *The Wall Street Journal*, the key rules are the same: prepare your points, inform yourself about whom you're really addressing, fashion quoteworthy statements, practice working your points into an interview, and don't cop an attitude, lie, or evade. Very few interviews will appear to be daunting experiences if you have your own agenda and are prepared to employ the skill set you've learned here to prosecute that agenda. Next up, we'll discuss some of the skills you'll need for radio interview mastery, and we'll look at the challenges and opportunities of a Skype interview.

ON THE AIR AND ON THE WEB: RADIO & SKYPE INTERVIEWS

When I joined ABC in 1968, the news division had a prodigious radio operation, staffed by highly professional and dedicated men and women. ABC News had divided its many radio affiliates into four mini-networks and the operation churned out four newscasts an hour, twenty-four hours a day, seven days a week. ABC Radio News tailored its four newscasts to different types of radio stations, ranging from the quick-paced, hip, and contemporary to the more serious information outlets.

Later, when I was executive producer of "Good Morning America," which was before CNN was even a gleam in Ted Turner's eye, there were only three national television networks doing news so I had in my office the obligatory three silent TV sets monitoring ABC, CBS, and NBC. But I also installed an ABC News radio line which I used to turn up to full volume six or eight times a day so I could hear a good summary of the latest top news. Summary is the key word here. Those broadcasts were highly compressed news, a succession of very short stories featuring soundbites that were even shorter than those in television newscasts. Hourly radio newscasts remain to this day ultra-short form journalism, but now a lot of stations do no newscasts at all. Information and talk stations are at the other end of the spectrum; many feature long interviews and expansive, detailed stories that can rival in content even a medium length newspaper article. National Public Radio's "Morning Edition" and the evening drive time "All Things Considered" are two shows that represent the best in the radio medium. But even the on-the-hour and on-the-half-hour newscasts on these shows are short form journalism. Most larger cities have at least one all-news radio station; outlets that churn out news twenty-four hours a day, but their stock in trade is the short, headline-style story, not the in-depth piece featuring substantial explanations, comprehensive soundbites, and contemplative analysis. Also, all-news stations repeat stories a lot because they know that there is substantial audience churn, with listeners tuning in for short bursts of information and then quickly tuning out. The all-news stations are voracious consumers of content and need a lot of material to stuff that 24/7 pipeline. If you are going to be part of the stuffing your remarks need to be extremely concise and pithy.

RADIO INTERVIEWS

Many spokespersons fail to differentiate between the broadcast media. While radio shares some similarities with television, the differences are important.

RADIO IS NOT TELEVISION
WITH THE PICTURE TURNED OFF

Let's deal with the fundamentals that all radio interviews share: no pictures and no reread factor. Radio is unlike any other medium because it is the only one that offers its audience no visual help at all. In a radio interview you have your words and nothing else. The listener can't see your sarcastic smile, your raised eyebrow, your happy grin. You are a disembodied voice.

As with the television viewer, the radio listener has no way of going back in the story and checking out what a spokesperson said or who he represents. What the listener hears initially is what she takes away. It's up to you to enable her to comprehend the first time around so make your soundbites accessible and memorable. It is a rule of all media mastery that you speak clearly, simply, and in short but complete sentences. Nowhere is that rule as critical as it is in radio. And add another mandate: You need to speak slowly enough for listeners to hear and understand you.

ENERGY IS RADIO'S EQUIVALENT
OF TELEVISION'S PICTURES

Speaking slowly does not mean speaking listlessly. On radio, you should energize your voice and give it character and color. You have only that one tool, your voice, to capture the listener's attention. Make your voice commanding by using inflection and stresses, not by talking at machine-gun speed. You can sound energetic even when you are speaking slowly enough for the most preoccupied listener to absorb what you're saying. A lot of professional radio personalities achieve vocal energy by acting out as they speak or read. That is, they grimace and gesticulate with exaggerated movement. To brighten their speech, they do something old radio pros call "putting teeth in it."

Putting teeth in a line means delivering it with a huge smile on your face. It looks ridiculous but sounds great. And, since it's not TV, no one sees the jack-o'-lantern grin. Try it. Record yourself on your smart phone reading a line with a normal facial expression and then reread it with a big smile on your face. When you play back the audio, you'll hear that smile.

Many stations, especially on the AM band, have initiated all-talk formats. There are sports talk radio stations, political talk radio stations, business talk radio stations, and general information radio stations. The trade publications call the talk radio stations "yakkers." A substantial number of the yakkers, especially those featuring political talk, employ hosts who seem perpetually angry about something. As angry as the talk jockeys are, their audience members seem to be angrier; at least those who phone in manifest even more volcanic fury than the hosts. The only thing these listeners like better than a heated argument is a verbal assault by the gab jock on someone with whom they disagree. For our purposes, talk radio falls into two categories: the listener-interrupted monologue and the listener-participation interview. In the former, the host delivers a commentary on the day's events and may field questions and comments from listeners. These shows rarely have guests and do no interviews. On the listener-participation interview shows, the host grills the guest and then throws the questioning open to the audience. An upside of these shows is the length of time they accord a guest. Frequently there is only one booking in a half hour segment of the show so there's really a lot of time to expound your views. The downside is that these shows are looking for action, drama, and conflict; in other words, a loud, emotional argument. To these shows, there is nothing like angry, hysterical shouting to attract and hold an audience.

Even if you aren't booked as a guest on a radio show, it is possible to book yourself if there's a call-in component. Simply by phoning in to the station, you can get yourself some air time. Talk jockeys will normally permit a caller to make a single statement or ask a single question so you can't go into one of these situations expecting to leave behind four or five agenda points. But there's no reason why you can't slip in one, or even two if you're graceful about it. Just remember, you must do all the branding yourself: "I work for Ynot Corporation and we're totally in support of…." In general there is a screener selecting which calls will get on the air. Entice the screener to pass you along to the host by deploying an effective grabber when you talk to her. Often she'll put you in the queue for on-air and remind you to repeat the grabber once you're talking with the host.

Call-in shows that place a premium on conflict, don't offer full and complete discussions of issues. Radio programs that book guests — as opposed to the phone-in shows — will allow you to speak for a longer time, but before going on the show make sure you know about the host and his audience: it's important to remember that second commandment: Thou Shalt Know Thy Listener. That information is critical with talk radio programs because it is so easy to get sandbagged by the host and audience of a show you don't know. If a radio station calls to book you, find out whether you're going to be praised, fawned over, skewered, belittled, ridiculed, or assaulted. That information is key to your preparation. If you can't listen to a radio broadcast before your interview, check the Internet — most stations and programs have an online presence these days. If you can't find anything on the Internet, ask around and find someone knowledgable so you can prepare for what's coming.

I don't mean to give the impressions that *all* radio shows are audio replays of the Spanish Inquisition. Indeed, some are comparable to fan magazines, with host and listeners taking turns praising guests with whom they agree. But at the other end of the spectrum are some very tough hosts who enjoy the loyalty of loud and opinionated listeners.

Your principal defense against an anticipated onslaught of ridicule is your inalienable right to not do the show. No media outlet has subpoena power; none can compel you to submit to an interview. If you are certain that you are going to be subjected to unreasonable treatment, that you are not going to be permitted to make any points, that you are being booked only to be the target of scorn, decline the invitation. If they've already booked you and you learn belatedly that the experience will be an audio waterboarding, unbook yourself. Declining an invitation is easy; virtually all talk radio is live, so it's understandable if you have a conflicting appointment that prevents you from accepting an invitation to your own public beheading. In cases where you accept an invitation and then learn enough about the show to know you're going to be skewered, unbook yourself as early as possible so the show can find a replacement in plenty of time and not harbor too much resentment against you. There are any number of perfectly reasonable excuses for retracting your acceptance to appear: appointment conflicts, legal counsel recommendation, company or organization policy. While a television station might stage a dramatic confrontation between an opponent of yours and an empty chair meant to represent you, this gimmick doesn't work on radio. The worst that can happen is the talk jock will mention once or twice that you had accepted an invitation to appear and then changed your mind. After only a couple of repetitions this begins to sound petty and it's likely he will abandon the theme and move on to someone who is in the studio and available for his assault with a barrage of deadly questions.

Of course, if you are the sort of person who feels any publicity, no matter how adverse, is better than no publicity, go ahead and stick your neck out. You may win; you may not. In fact, by your own standards you may win even if a lot of listeners feel you've lost. When the syndicated Howard Stern radio show began airing in the Los Angeles market in the 1980s, I listened to the inaugural broadcast. Weight-loss guru Richard Simmons called in to congratulate Stern on his West Coast debut. Stern lashed into Simmons and kept up a stream of hateful, homophobic invective for what seemed like a cruel eternity. I remember thinking, "Hang up, Richard. Cut it off." But Simmons stayed the course, although Stern reduced him to tears. At the time I was supervising producer of ABC-TV's "Home Show" and Richard was a frequent guest on the show. When I next saw him, I told Simmons I had heard the broadcast and I felt Stern had treated him shabbily. "Oh," said Simmons, "he always does that when I'm on his show." Always? This had happened before and Simmons came back for more? To Richard Simmons, the humiliation was worth it because it gave him an opportunity to reach out to the overweight people among Stern's listeners.

TALK RADIO PREPARATION

Once you make up your mind to accept an invitation to appear on a radio talk show, find out the circumstances of your appearance. Ask if you'll be the only guest and the length of your segment. Also, ask how long you'll be talking with the host before he takes listener calls. Armed with that knowledge try to get all of your message points into the host's interview before he opens the phones to the public. If you can manage that, you will set the agenda and the callers will be more likely to address your points with their questions and comments. Once the calls start coming in, remember to keep your agenda at the forefront. Often callers don't ask questions but use their time on the air to make statements. If a caller agrees with you, endorses what you said, or praises you, thank him and reiterate the point to reinforce it. This is not the time for saying, "Aw shucks, thanks a lot, caller." It's a time to put your message in audio boldface. If the caller opposes one of your points, I have a three-step variation on our four-step bridging technique.

INTERVIEW BRIDGING
Short form answer
Build a Bridge
Agenda Point
Shut Up!

RADIO CALL-IN VARIATION
Disagree at Once
Agenda Point
Shut Up!
(There is no bridge)

¶ **Disagree at Once.** There was no question; instead, the caller made a statement, so you don't have to come up with an answer. Your simple response, "I disagree with that," both challenges the caller's statement and builds the equivalent of a bridge. "You're dead wrong," is even stronger than "I disagree," and sometimes in the rough-and-tumble world of talk radio, you'll want to be extremely assertive.

¶ **State your agenda point.** Do this forcefully and quickly. Don't repeat the caller's assertions; that just emphasizes *his* point of view by giving it more airtime. Get your Positive Message Statement into the listeners' ears early. Doing this resets the agenda from the caller's to your own. If the host is on the caller's side, he may try to shoehorn in a question sympathetic to the caller's point of view. If he does, then use the interview technique and build a bridge from that question to another of your agenda points.

¶ **Shut Up.** In an interview setting the final rule was to shut up — that is, to avoid bringing your answer back to his question as in, "So that's why this is not a disaster waiting to happen." In response to an assertion from a radio caller, you want to do the same thing; you want to end your statement on your own message point, not return to his.

Let me demonstrate this technique with something truly controversial and highly improbable: Ynot Corporation's plan to build a nuclear-fueled electrical power plant in the New Jersey Meadowlands, just outside New York City. This project is going to be a tough sell so you have worked up four strong Positive Message Statements for your agenda and you've kept them short and simple:

1. The plant will be nonpolluting. Unlike fossil fuel plants, nuclear facilities emit neither particulates, like soot and ash, nor greenhouse gases, like carbon dioxide. Ynot's plant will neither pollute nor contribute to global warming. (30 words, two sentences.)

2. The plant will reduce U.S. dependence on foreign sources of energy. At current import prices, an oil-fired plant generating the same amount of electricity will enrich foreign oil suppliers by more than $200 million every year. (26 words, two sentences.)

3. The plant will be safe to the point of being foolproof. The technology used in the Ynot Meadowlands plant has a proven, half-century safety record in nuclear-powered U.S. Navy vessels. (22 words, one sentence.)

4. The plant will save consumers money. Customers will save money. Technology advancements mean Ynot Meadowlands will supply cheaper electricity to consumers over the plant's life than a similar capacity oil, coal or natural gas facility. (30 words, Two sentences.)

Despite your positive messages, this is going to be an emotional issue. People remember Chernobyl, the Soviet nuclear plant that melted down in 1986, releasing dangerous levels of radioactivity. In addition, they have a fear-provoking example closer to home: Three Mile Island, which the media and nuclear critics portrayed as an American Chernobyl, although there was no significant release of any radioactive material at that Pennsylvania plant. More recently, California's San Onofre Nuclear Generating Station was shut down because of leaks of radioactive water and and a tsunami crippled Japan's Fukushima electric power plant and caused dangerous levels of radiation to contaminate a large swatch of land. Because this is a hot-button issue, you have armed yourself with facts and figures: the difference between the poorly engineered and shoddily maintained Chernobyl plant and American designs, the fact that no one was harmed at Three Mile Island, the number of U.S. Navy ships powered by nuclear reactors, the fact that France safely generates most of its electricity using nuclear reactors, and the U.S. Department of Energy's record for guarding spent nuclear waste against terrorists and other potential thieves.

You're on a radio call-in show. The host has grilled you for a while, and the phones are flashing because you're dealing with such a controversial matter. The talk jock takes his first call. In a heated and emotional tone, the caller says: "I live near the Meadowlands and no one's gonna put a nuclear power plant in my backyard! If the government's too chicken-livered to stop 'em, I'll go to court with my neighbors and tie this up 'til the cows come home. And if the court gives you a go-ahead, we'll lie down on the highway and block the construction trucks. If you build what you're proposing you'll be exposing my kids to dangerous radioactivity. I don't see you living next door to a nuclear power plant with your kids."

Now you're going to respond with the "Disagree at Once, State Your PMS, Shut Up" technique. The most logical message to work in here is your third one: The plant will be safe to the point of being foolproof.

There was no question, just a frightened and pugnacious statement. So here's a response that uses our three steps: "That's not the case at all. [Disagree at once - without repeating his point of view] Safety is our number one priority. That's why we designed this plant to be safe; safe to the point of being foolproof. The U.S. Navy has used this same technology aboard four hundred ships over fifty years, without a single nuclear mishap. Ynot's plant will be just as safe for our workers and neighbors. [State your agenda point and shut up]" By using this technique, you have not gotten bogged down in a discussion of his children's safety — an emotional approach on his part which will have great sway with the public since it appeals to fear — and you've kept it short and simple. The "pull quote" part of your answer, beginning with "The U.S. Navy," is 30 words long, expressed in two sentences and is comprehensible at the sixth grade level. (Remember, in ordinary media encounters you aim no higher than tenth grade comprehension, the national average grade level. But with emotional issues like this one, you gear comprehension levels down to the sixth grade level because even the most sophisticated adult processes fear-inducing arguments like a frightened 11-year-old.)

RADIO VIRTUES

Let's say you are approached to do a radio interview with a talent you are reasonably sure will not assault you with a barrage of deadly questions, one who will permit you to get in your points during a vigorous but fundamentally fair interrogation. This is an opportunity to get some message points out, but you want to be sure you emerge from the experience a radio saint, not a radio sinner. There four virtues you need to know about to be a competent radio communicator.

RADIO VIRTUES

BREVITY
ENERGY
SIMPLICITY
BRANDING

¶ **Brevity.** In Chapter 4, I wrote about the need to keep answers short and simple. In no medium is this more important than in radio. Let's deal with the short part first. You already know that radio is a non-visual medium without a reread factor. A very long statement can sound like a speech or a sermon. While an interview is not a conversation, it masquerades as one because it is much more interesting for a listener to eavesdrop on a conversation than it is to listen to a speech. In a tough interview, many of us have an impulse to filibuster, reasoning, "If I keep talking, he can't ask me more questions." On the radio, speaking at excessive length not only may fail to forestall other questions, but also may spur the interviewer to ask tougher questions. And even if it doesn't, your long-winded answers are sure to frustrate listeners and cause their attention to wander. Once an answer has gone on too long, many radio interviewers will throw manners to the wind and interrupt you with the next question.

So speak in short sentences and short paragraphs: one thought to a sentence, and one PMS to an answer. Brevity is not "Yes" and "No." As I wrote earlier, "Yes" and "No" are not answers but are the beginning of answers.

¶ **Energy.** Silence is the deadliest thing in radio. Just as nature abhors a vacuum, radio abhors silence. Think about this: if you were channel surfing on television, tuned to channel five, and there was nothing on-screen — no picture, no sound — you'd move on to another channel. Similarly, a listener hunting through the radio dial and hearing no talk, no music, nothing but the "sound of silence," assumes that there's no station and moves on. Radio interviewers know this and don't want to lose the station surfers, so if you are silent for too long after a question, it's likely your interviewer will begin talking to fill the void. When he's talking, he's using the medium's most precious commodity — airtime — and you are not. You can't deliver your message when he's talking.

And when you do talk, you need to do it energetically. Vocal energy is the anthesis of silence. I've already written a little bit about the need to make your voice interesting because in radio there are no supporting visuals. An energetic voice is an interesting voice. Your energy conveys enthusiasm for your agenda; your level of enthusiasm can be infectious. Don't confuse energy with speed. An energetic voice is not a fast-talking voice, rather it is a voice that employs coloration, emphasis, brightness not speed. If you go fast, you may qualify to join the Fast Talkers of America Club, but you'll leave the audience in your verbal dust. Listen to the really good radio communicators: they stress words a little unnaturally for everyday conversation, they change the pace of their delivery, and they vary their volume, raising it slightly to put in boldface words or phrases they want to emphasize. I was in the audio booth one day while the late Howard Cosell did his two minutes on "Good Morning America," and I watched the volume needles as they did a wild dance. Cosell would speak very quietly and then suddenly raise his voice to a near shout for emphasis. His pace, too, would vary from very slow to moderately fast — but never so fast you couldn't catch his words. Known for his television appearances, Cosell — like most sports booth announcers — was really an audio performer, and he used energy to make his voice interesting. He didn't have the resonant bass often associated with radio voices, but he used his reedy, nasal voice as well as anyone in the medium. You don't have to sound like James Earl Jones to interest a radio listener. While it takes a lot of practice to get to a career announcer's stage of professionalism, you can do what they do on a more modest scale by varying your tone and your speed, by gesturing in an exaggerated way and by coloring your voice by "putting teeth" into your words from time to time.

¶ **Simplicity.** With no reread factor as there is in print and no graphics assist as there is in television, radio listeners get one brief shot at comprehending what you're saying. In media training sessions I used to tell participants that rather than "dumb down" their answers, just pretend to be talking to their uncle across the table at Thanksgiving dinner and speak at the appropriate level for him to understand. Simplicity is not necessarily dumbing down what you say; it's just making sure that the audience has the opportunity to grasp your meaning. That means simplifying as much as you can without changing the meaning of what you're saying. Earlier I mentioned the arrangement we had at "Good Morning America" with the author Isaac Asimov, who filled in when a guest failed to show up. Asimov was a science fiction author of wide renown, but he was also a great popularizer of science fact, and many of his books shed light on scientific mysteries for the general public. To me he was always at the top of his game when he was able to make comprehensible to our audience a complex scientific theory or development. He kept it simple, explaining things in layman's terms and using examples whenever possible. But he never condescended to the audience. That's the secret of simplicity.

¶ **Branding.** Just before I began writing this chapter I listened to a radio interview with a British female pop singer. Like many listeners, I joined the interview in progress. During the portion of the interview I heard — a good three or four minutes — neither she nor the interviewer ever identified her or her band, although both made reference to "the band." Nor did either of them name her album. At one point the interviewer said, "I understand the version of the CD that's been issued in this country has three additional tracks on it that weren't on the British original." Now how much effort would it have taken to insert the name of the CD in that statement? "That's right," Ms. Unknown said, missing an opportunity to correct the interviewer's omission, "I'm very excited about it because when they cut one of those songs out of the U.K. version I sat down and cried."

It is the job of the radio host to identify his interview subject for her listeners. A good radio interviewer does that with regularity — every third or fourth question.

A good radio interviewer will also help you brand. She'll not only give your name, but also will mention why you're on the show. Terry Gross on NPR's "Fresh Air" will say from time to time, "We're talking with George Merlis, author of *Merlis on Media Mastery.*" And she'll ask questions like this: "George Merlis, in your book *Merlis on Media Mastery,* you contend that it's up to the guest to mention his brand during an interview. Why is this necessary?" But not every interviewer is that professional or conscientious, so it's up to you to do that branding. For instance, to a host who doesn't use the book name, I might say, "Well, my book, *Merlis on Media Mastery,* gives readers the tools they need to be the best guest on your show so that they can help entertain and inform your audience." If I say, "Well, *my book* gives readers the tools...." I am daring the listener to find the name of the book himself. Most won't bother trying.

Not too long ago I was media training a recording artist who asked me, "How do I get my name in if the radio interviewer never uses it. Won't that sound egotistical?" I explained to him that it was, indeed, a lot easier to work in a band's name (i.e. Maroon 5) than a solo artist's name (i.e. Adam Levine). It's also easier to work in a book title or a company's name than your personal moniker. For example, "Well, our band, Wolfbite blends the energy of...." comes to the tongue a lot easier than, "The Frank Ritchie sound is a blend of...." If you do talk about yourself in the third person, the listener may think you are speaking about someone else. I remember Diana Ross on "Good Morning America" beginning the answer to a David Hartman question along these lines, "Well, that wasn't the right career move for Diana Ross so....." And she kept talking about herself in the third person. In the control room we joked about the identity of the Diana Ross lookalike David was interviewing.

When he was running for president in 1996, Senator Bob Dole spoke often about "Bob Dole," as if he were discussing another person. Sen. Dole's practice — eschewing the pronoun "I" in favor of using his full name — invited ridicule and, among others, "Saturday Night Live" was only too happy to accept the invitation, casting one of its regulars as Bob Dole who used his name in virtually every sentence he uttered.

The easiest way to work your name into an interview is to quote someone else. "You know, it was a real honor when *Rolling Stone* wrote, 'Frank Ritchie is the new Elton John.'" Another way is to include yourself in a story: "I dropped my middle name, Philip, when I was 12 and became just Frank Richie." Obviously, you resort to these awkward strategies only if your interviewer fails to identify you.

SKYPE INTERVIEWS

Skype and similar technologies offer TV outlets a quick, cost-efficient way to add an otherwise unavailable interview to a story. Print outlets use Skype interviews for video in the website versions of stories. Skype — I'm using the brand name generically for all video phone technology — presents a few challenges and one big opportunity. Let me deal with the opportunity first.

Skype is an Open Book Test

Like a phone interview, a Skype Q&A is an open book test. You can write your agenda in a presentation or word processing application and have it on your computer screen in front of you. This would be my laptop screen for a Skype interview about Skype interviews:

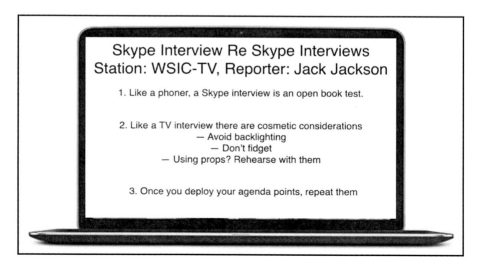

Skype Interview Re Skype Interviews
Station: WSIC-TV, Reporter: Jack Jackson

1. Like a phoner, a Skype interview is an open book test.

2. Like a TV interview there are cosmetic considerations
— Avoid backlighting
— Don't fidget
— Using props? Rehearse with them

3. Once you deploy your agenda points, repeat them

163

Because the camera is at the top of my laptop screen, I have my agenda in view throughout the interview, without ever having to look down at index cards, so it's unlikely the reporter or viewer will think I am using notes.

My third point on the screen is this: once you deploy your agenda points, repeat them. In any open book interview it's pretty easy to work in your agenda very quickly. It's incumbent on you to then go back and revisit that agenda when you answer the reporter's subsequent questions. If you stray from your agenda, you invite the reporter to write a story that strays, too.

Skype Challenges

While staying on message is not unique to a Skype interview, overseeing the production aspects of your interview is unique. When a TV crew comes to your office to set up an interview, its members will move furniture, banish reflective objects from the background, perhaps offer a little powder to take the shine off your brow and light your office with professional skill. A pro sets up the camera, makes sure you are properly framed and keeps an eye in the viewfinder throughout the interview so he can follow you if you move and can shoot close-ups of any props or graphics you may deploy. With a Skype interview, *you* are the camera person, makeup artist, lighting director and prop master. It's likely none of these are your chosen craft. No one expects a Skype interview to look as if it had been lit by an Emmy-winning lighting director, but make every effort to insure the image is as good as the little camera embedded in your computer or phone can make it and that the audio is superior to what you get from the cheap microphones embedded in those devices.

Since one picture is worth a thousand words, take a look at this screen shot of a Skype interview:

Self-explanatory, isn't it? Don't set your computer up in an area where the light behind you is stronger than the light in front of you. (Unless you're doing it on purpose — as an anonymous whistle-blower, for example.) The Skype image below is good:

It was posted on the web by Skype itself, so you can bet there was professional lighting and makeup involved. Still, it gives us a clear indication of what a good image looks like. The woman is evenly lit — which you can do with a pair of soft light lamps placed on either side of your laptop or computer monitor — the background is not distracting and her eye line is good. If you are using a camera embedded in the frame of a laptop, you can adjust the angle — and your eye line — by tilting the screen forward and back. With a desktop computer, you'll have to move yourself up or down to make that sort of adjustment. You want the camera at or a little above eye level, but not so high that you have to thrust out your chin to see it comfortably. If you can come up with an appropriate backdrop, that's even better than the white wall behind the woman. A repeat pattern is a good backdrop — the logo or seal of your organization printed repeatedly over a contrasting (but not too bright) color. Any company or organization with a competent graphics department can turn out a logo repeat on a large sheet of paper, paste it to a foam board and bring it to any office in the building or on the campus for a Skype interview.

Other Skype Tips:

Look at the camera, not down at notes or up for divine inspiration.

In most interviews you want your head and shoulders to fill the screen. But if you are going to hold up props, you'll want to give yourself a little more room, so move back to insure the props fill but do not overflow the screen.

If you are going to use props, practice with them. Move very slowly — as if you are under water — so that viewers can see them. Hold them in front of the camera for what seems like far too long. Then hold them there a few more seconds. Move them out of camera range slowly, don't jerk them away.

Avoid swivel chairs — if you're sitting in one, you are likely to twist from side to side and appear nervous.

Skype Audio

Microphones built into laptops, tablets and phones are adequate for a phone call but fall short of broadcast audio standards. The best remedy: place yourself in a quiet room, turn off fans, air conditioners or other noisy distractions and, if at all possible, use an external microphone. There is a vast array of external microphones on the market, many priced below $100. Skype's website lists several, but shop around, the Skype price may not be the best price. If you do use an external microphone, you may have to change your preferences or settings to insure your device does not default to its built-in microphone.

In the next chapter, I'll review another occasion where you can have your PMSs in front of you — a news conference — and I'll deal with the unique challenges of performing on-camera demonstrations.

CHAPTER 10

WHEN YOU'RE IN CHARGE: ON-CAMERA DEMONSTRATIONS & NEWS CONFERENCES

In two instances, you know that the media will definitely address your agenda: news conferences and on-camera television demonstrations. In the latter, you are booked solely to explain and/or demonstrate your product (I include as products how-to books, such as cookbooks). Therefore, the entire segment will accommodate your agenda and you have more control over the situation than you would in a conventional broadcast or print interview.

In a news conference, reporters and camera crews come to a venue at your invitation to hear the news you will make. In other words, your agenda has drawn them, so you are in charge — at least at the beginning. Later in this chapter, I'll show you how to remain in charge throughout a news conference, even one called in reaction to events beyond your control. After reading this chapter, you'll have specific tools to help you maintain your cool and handle even the most challenging news conferences or on-camera demonstrations.

ON-CAMERA DEMONSTRATIONS

For our purposes, a demonstration can be something as simple as voicing-over some prepared video you've supplied to the program, or it may be holding up a prop and showing it to the camera. More involved demonstrations are actual how-to segments like food preparation, repair, design, or technical projects. Here are the basic tips for any physical demonstration before a TV camera:

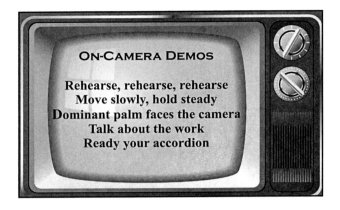

ON-CAMERA DEMOS

Rehearse, rehearse, rehearse
Move slowly, hold steady
Dominant palm faces the camera
Talk about the work
Ready your accordion

¶ **Rehearse, rehearse, rehearse.** Our fourth command-ment of interviews is practice, practice, practice. Well, for demonstrations, rewrite that as rehearse, rehearse, rehearse. At home or in the office, practice doing the demonstration at differ-ent lengths: two minutes, three minutes, four minutes, and — may you be this lucky — five minutes. Prepare all your pieces, ingredients, and tools beforehand. Lay them out in a logical or-der so the camera follows them left to right (meaning they are right to left for you because you are facing the camera). Use a video camera and record your rehearsal. First time through use a wide shot to simulate the TV studio's master shot. On your sec-ond run-through, focus on the close-ups, so you can see if they are working. If at all possible, feed the output of your video camera into a TV set so you can monitor your movements as you go.*

¶ **Move slowly, hold steady.** Jan Rifkinson, the first director of "Good Morning America," used to tell guests who were doing demos, "Move as if you are under water," which is a sound piece

---

* Don't be thrown by your likeness in a monitor: TV is a *direct* image, while we are used to seeing ourselves in a mirror, which is actually a *reverse* image. When you move your right hand to the right the monitor makes it appear as if you are moving your left hand to the left. The television image is the accurate one be-cause it is another person's view of us.

of advice. Visualize how water resistance in a lake or pond keeps you from making rapid movements. That's exactly how you should move when you are doing a demo for TV. Close-up cameras have difficulty following rapid movements; you may yank items right out of the camera's frame if you move them too fast. Even if the items stay in frame, rapid movement may seem like a blur to the viewer at home.

The close-up camera exaggerates any sort of motion, so if you hold something in a shaky or unsteady way, it's hard for viewers to see it. This is especially critical if there is anything they have to read — such as a book jacket or CD cover. The easiest way to hold an item steady is to have your hands resting on the table or counter while you hold it; the solid base on which you're resting your hands will keep them from moving. If you must hold an item up, try holding it with both hands, elbows bent 90 degrees and locked tight against your ribs. This gives your forearms and hands support and rigidity.

If you think you've held something in place for enough time, you're probably wrong. Extend the hold by at least 50 percent more time. You do this to let the camera catch up with you. If you hold up a book, a CD, or a plate of freshly prepared asparagus and take it down quickly, the closeup camera may not have enough time to find it, frame up on it, and get it into focus. In the studio, before you begin, ask if they'll place a monitor in your line of sight so you can sneak a peek and make sure that your item is on camera long enough for viewers to identify it. (A demo is the *only* TV appearance during which it's O.K. to look at a monitor.)

¶ **Dominant palm faces the camera.** If you are standing at a demonstration counter with your elbows bent and your hands outstretched, palms perpendicular to the counter, the close-up camera should be on your left side if you are right-handed and on your right side if you are left-handed. In other words, the close-up camera should be shooting *into* the palm of your dominant hand. If you are wondering why, let's take the case of a right-handed guest doing a demonstration. If the close-up camera is shooting from his right, the back of his dominant hand is going to cover the details of the work he is doing.

It is surprising how many television directors don't know this very basic rule for shooting close-ups of demos. You can't direct your own segment, so what can you do about it? I suggest that during the run-through you ask which is the close-up camera and, if it's on the wrong side, gently point out to the director or to the stage manager that you are right-handed (or left-handed) and your right (or left) hand will block the close-up camera. If there is no run-through, before you go on ask the stage manager which is the close-up camera. If it is on the wrong side, move even more slowly and periodically take your hand away from the work so the camera can get an unencumbered shot. Alternatively, you can favor your non-dominant hand if it has sufficient dexterity.

¶ **Talk while you work, but talk about the work.** As bad as directors who don't know where to place their close-up cameras are hosts who ask you off-point questions while you are doing a demonstration. Imagine you are about to show the host how to score a mango. As you begin, you mention that the mango is the most popular fruit in the world, even though it is far less popular in the United States. Picking up on the word fruit, she asks you whether the tomato is a fruit or a vegetable. If you answer the question while continuing to score the mango, the viewers lose out on having you narrate while you demonstrate — the most basic element of a demonstration. The solution: stop scoring that mango while you answer the question and then segue back to the demonstration and talk about what you are doing as you do it.

¶ **Ready your accordion.** Just before you go on, you may be told you'll have four minutes. You go into your four-minute mode — but you're only two-thirds of the way in and the stage manager is frantically signaling the talent to wrap it up. This happens all the time on live shows, where segments after the first or second act are often squeezed because those earlier acts ran long. When the talent, responding to the stage manager, says to you, "Now, moving along, how do we get to the final product?" you need to accordion your demo. If you rehearsed, rehearsed, and rehearsed some more and if, in these rehearsals, you ran through your demonstration at a variety of lengths, you can easily move to the shortest version for the remaining steps. You may feel cheated by this rush job, but you won't appear flustered on the air.

You can deliver effective messages in a demonstration. When you're doing something on camera, you command the viewer's attention. Just remember that in addition to the "show" there's the "tell." You want to work your PMSs into your description of what you're doing.

News Conferences

A news conference is an opportunity to reach many media outlets simultaneously. But it also presents a singular set of challenges. More about those in a moment; first let's consider when and why you might want to convene a news conference.

A variety of circumstances call for news conferences. While some government agencies hold press briefings daily or weekly, we are more concerned here with the event- or product-oriented news conference. Companies and organizations typically hold these sessions to announce new products, reveal major economic plans, or respond to developments either good or bad that may impact their earnings or their place in a community. Nonprofits often call news conferences to announce new initiatives, fundraising activity, or developments made possible by their efforts. In times of labor strife — or impending strife — it is not unusual for both labor and management to set out their positions before the public in a series of dueling news conferences. A news conference sends the signal that your story is more important than the ordinary grist for reportorial mills; that it demands the news media's in-person attention.

Sometimes, news conferences are conducted when there is no news; they are designed simply to keep speculation and bad information from creating an inaccurate public impression. During the 2002 sniper attacks in the Washington, DC, area there were daily news conferences, usually led by Charles Moose, the police chief of Montgomery Country, Maryland. At many of these sessions, Chief Moose had no real news to report, but he kept briefing the media on a regular basis to let the nervous public know police agencies were investigating the shootings and were following all leads. By conducting such news conferences, Chief Moose could also rebut speculation and dampen rumors. While reporters might grumble that there had been "no news," if the press briefing prevented dissemination of speculation and rumor, it served the purposes both of the police and of journalism by keeping inaccurate information in check. On other occasions Chief Moose used news conferences to try to communicate with the snipers. In those instances, the conferences themselves became part of the story.

WHAT TO BRING TO A NEWS CONFERENCE

Give the assembled press supporting documentation and visuals. If you are announcing a new product or service, include thorough descriptions in the handout materials. Lay out in detail the most minute and technical details in these handouts. You should give the media photographs, diagrams, and video files to enhance your presentation. The best video to distribute is a B-roll package — the elements a reporter can use to make a story. In most cases, samples of the product should be available for the reporters to work with; this often yields first-person accounts which the public may view as impartial third party endorsements.

If a news conference kicks off an event, you may want to supply both background video and a live video feed. One of the most successful public relations projects I ever did involved B-roll and a live video feed. Honda was about to ship to Japan the first batch of its Accord coupes, which were made only in the company's plant in Ohio. It was historic; for the first time Japanese-branded, American-built cars were being exported in large numbers to Japan, rather than visa versa. We staged the news conference on a pier in Portland, Oregon. We supplied the assembled media with B-roll of the manufacture of the autos, and we covered the news conference live with three strategically placed cameras and fed the event worldwide via satellite. The payoff came when the Accord coupes rolled out of the parking lot, up a ramp, and onto the ship that would take them across the Pacific. Hundreds of TV stations downlinked and used some of our coverage, as did numerous broadcasters in Japan and two of the three U.S. broadcast network nightly newscasts.

The lesson here is you'll really enhance your news conference if you give the attending television outlets additional video to take away. Newspapers, too, will use rolling video in their online editions and they can use other visuals like stills, charts, and graphs. For radio, if you're dealing with a product or project that involves sound of any kind, distribute audio files with those sounds. You may also want to include in the audio handout material soundbites from persons unavailable at the news conference.

NEWS CONFERENCES ARE NOT INTERVIEWS

As anyone who has watched a presidential news conference on live television knows, a gaggle of press can be a lot
tougher than a single reporter. In a one-on-one interview, you
have the ability to research the individual reporter beforehand.
And in such an interview the reporter usually builds a line of
questioning, much as a writer would build a story. She follows
up on answers and there is an organic growth to the exchange.
Not so in a news conference where there will likely be too many
reporters for you to assess them in advance and where the questions don't logically flow in an organic building process. Because you are confronting multiple reporters with multiple agendas in a news conference, you need to think on your feet. Fortunately, if you've brought an agenda to the session, your thought
process usually is, "How do I bridge from that question to an
agenda point?" Also in news conferences there is an almost inevitable herd instinct operating. Dodge a question in a one-on-
one interview and the reporter may or may not press the point.
Dodge a question in front of a dozen reporters and at least a few
of them will be waving eagerly to get your attention so they can
put your feet back to the fire.

In a one-on-one interview, you likely will have a warmup
period, which you can use to plant seeds for questions that will
serve your agenda. There is no warmup in a news conference.
Also, you may have reporters representing the most sophisticated
publications and representatives of mass market tabloids, so
knowing your listener is more challenging.

Your news conference attendees may represent a variety of
media as well. There will be television cameras, still photographers, print reporters, bloggers and radio correspondents. You
may be speaking into a forest of microphones, and you may be
facing not one or two but half a dozen bright television lights and
the repeated blinding flashes of still cameras. Instead of the
conversational tones you've come to expect from one-on-one
interviewers, the reporters may shout their questions at you. Because they are in competition with each other to get their own
questions asked and because they know that the time available to
them is finite, their manners may go by the board.

A news conference poses a host of challenges for you:
How do you answer a rude, shouted question? Do you adopt the
cosmetic style and posture of a television interview? Do you

keep your answers simple, even though some reporters represent sophisticated and specialized media outlets? How do you keep one reporter from dominating the session by asking a string of follow-up questions or making a speech? How do you end a news conference if the flow of questions shows no sign of abating? How do you deal with redundant questions?

Despite the challenges, a news conference is a unique opportunity to reach multiple media outlets — and their audiences — with great economy of time. A few simple techniques will help you maximize that opportunity.

You might be conflicted: should you speak to the lowest common denominator or should you tailor each answer to the particular audience served by each reporter? Attempting the latter puts an undue burden on you; you'll have to keep changing your tone and level of sophistication throughout the news conference, and you'll have to know the sophistication level of every media outlet represented in the room. Moreover, if you answer any question with the most sophisticated audience in mind, you run the risk of having the same question asked again by someone who represents a mass-market outlet and wants your answer in language his audience can comprehend. So for a news conference, go with the basics. Oftentimes the simple answer will suffice for all the media present. For example, I do a lot of work prepping scientists for news briefings. The range of reporters at the conference may run from *USA Today* to the journal, *Science*. Clearly, the *Science* readers are a lot more sophisticated about the subject than the average *USA Today* reader. I tell my clients to use the *USA Today* answers and then, if the *Science* reporter needs additional information, he can usually glean it from the printed handout material that you distribute at the news conference. Address the oral part of the news conference to the mass audience. Sophisticated supporting documents may satisfy the specialists who need a more advanced level of detail. An added benefit is that various publications — even those catering to the mass audience — may post the more sophisticated material from your handouts on their web sites as a service for those who might want or need such data.

OPENING REMARKS: YOU'RE IN CONTROL

Your dread of a single reporter may multiply many times over when you face a horde of them in a news conference. But remember this: the reporters are attending in response to your invitation and that means they are interested in your agenda. When you announced your news conference you told the media you were going to make news. That news was sufficiently interesting to draw their attendance. You have initial control over the agenda because you've told them, usually in very general terms, what the announcement is about. ("Sen. Goodhue will announce his plans concerning the presidential election," "The Ynot Corporation is going to announce the first major innovation in the Bumblepuppy product line in three years," "Stupendous Foundation is going to announce a major grant in the health care sector.") The first thing you do in a news conference is take the podium and make opening remarks that further define the agenda. Never begin a news conference without making an opening statement. If you don't take advantage of that opportunity, you are yielding control of the agenda right at the start.

Before the media assemble, place your opening remarks and your Positive Message Statements — in bullet points on separate index cards — on the lectern, so you'll be ready to use them during the session.

Don't read the first or last sentences of your opening remarks; deliver them from memory. If you begin by engaging the room — and not staring down at your notes — and conclude your introductory remarks the same way, you will command the attention of your audience. Make your opening and closing sentences assertive and quoteworthy. Television is more likely to use remarks addressed to the audience than those read from the lectern. So start and finish your opening statement with strong stuff that you've rehearsed, memorized, and can deliver with vigorous authority. Here's an example: "Today, Ynot Corporation is announcing a major breakthrough in the production of environmentally friendly home fuel cells — a breakthrough that will allow every home in America to generate its own electricity at a fraction of the price we now pay for power." And, similarly, this last sentence: "The Ynot Fuel cell will help reduce our dependence on foreign energy sources and, at the same time, significantly cut air pollution and fight greenhouse gas emissions." If you can deliver lines like these without referring to your notes, they will likely wind up on TV.

DRESS THE LECTERN

Earlier I advised placing your PMSs on the lectern in front of you at a news conference. An occasional glance down will refresh your memory about which one you can deploy to answer a given question, and that gesture does not look unnatural. It will look peculiar, however, if you address your answers to the lectern and not to the reporters in the audience. Use the cards only for reference; do not read them. It's a good idea to reduce your agenda to bullet points so you won't even be tempted to read them. As with a phoner, if each point is on a separate index card, you can flip that card after you deploy the message point. This encourages you to work in all your agenda messages. What to do with notes and index cards at the end of the session? Leave them there on the lectern but detail an associate to clean up after you. Why plant them on the lectern before you begin and why leave them there at the end? I'm sure you've seen speakers approach a lectern and, as I call it, get dressed.   They walk up, fumble for their notes in a pocket — or, worse yet, in a briefcase. Then they organize the notes on the lectern, all the while looking down.   Once organized, they begin reading the notes without engaging the room. Approaching a lectern this way does not command attention or inspire confidence; a speaker who is so dependent on his written materials loses some of his credibility. And that's why it's a good idea to dress the lectern in advance, stride up behind it, and begin with that memorized opening line. At the end, of the news conference, after the Q&A, don't waste time and diminish your command of the moment by picking up all the detritus on the lectern; leave that chore to an associate to take care of after you have left the stage. It's important, though, that *someone* round up that material; you don't want to leave notes where a snooping reporter might snatch them up and use them to write a snide story about how you prepared for the news conference.

ADDITIONAL NEWS CONFERENCE TIPS

¶ **Don't rest your elbows on the lectern.** It looks sloppy and on television sends the wrong body language message. Also, don't grasp the lectern. If you do you're unlikely to use your hands to gesture. I've seen speakers hold on to the lectern as if it were a lifeboat lowered into the icy waters of the Atlantic when the *Titanic* sank. The lectern is there for your notes, not to hold up your frail body. If you want to command the news media's respect and attention, stand on your own two feet.

¶ **Dress the room correctly.** How many television stories have you seen where the only graphic in a speech or news conference was the name of the hotel posted on the lectern? You are not there to promote a hotel; you are there to promote a cause, a product, a position, or a policy, so bring signage to hang on the lectern and, if possible, more signage to hang behind you. It may be the corporate logo, it may be the name of the cause, product, position, or policy. Regardless, visual aids help. Politicians cover the walls behind them with "wallpaper" that features a repeat graphic, usually with a campaign or party symbol and a brief slogan. No matter how the speaker is photographed, the wallpaper appears in the background, clearly legible.

¶ **Rehearse with media stand-ins.** It's a good idea to run through the prepared portion of your news conference in the actual venue, using stand-ins for the media. This is particularly useful in helping you place and play to still and TV cameras; you want to be certain the cameras will have a good, clear shot of you at the lectern. I attended a news conference in Las Vegas where the American flag was downstage of the lectern, partially blocking the TV cameras' shot of the speaker. If the news conference organizers had taken the trouble to stand on the camera platform in advance, they would have seen that the flag blocked the cameras and they would have moved it.

¶ **Initiate the question period.** At the end of your prepared statement, call for questions. Set a time limit on the Q&A session: "I'll now take questions for fifteen minutes." This puts everyone on notice that you are beginning a limited-duration Q&A session and not an open forum for journalists to give their opinions. Any reporter who starts making a speech after you've given a finite length to the Q&A session is likely to be admonished into silence by his colleagues. In the event you do get a speechifier and his colleagues don't shut him up, you have control of the lectern and the microphone, so pick out a question in his rambling discourse and answer it. "I can see you're concerned about how we will distribute these fuel cells, and let me answer that." In other words, if no question is forthcoming, infer one.

¶ **Prime the pump if you need to.** On rare occasions, the reporters may be slow to raise their hands and ask the first question. If this happens, ask yourself a question. Phrase it this way, "I'm frequently asked about how we can deliver these fuel cells on the schedule we've announced." Then go on to answer it. Always ask yourself a question that enables one of your PMSs. It can even be one of the questions from your prepared list of hostile questions — one that you can answer with a deftly built bridge to a PMS. It's likely you're going to phrase the question in a far less hostile manner than a challenging journalist will and, by asking yourself the question, you've preempted the reporters from asking it. If a reporter does ask a variation of your tough first question, you can say, "I addressed that in answer to the first question." This technique is effective if a number of reporters feel compelled to ask you the same question. If you've already answered it, tell them that and move on; you need not answer the same question repeatedly.

¶ **Start with a "friend."** Obviously there's no need to prime the pump if the reporters jump at the opportunity to ask questions. In that case, it's a good policy to take your first question from a reporter who has treated you fairly in the past, because chances are she will do it again. Do not recognize for the first question someone who you know to be a skeptical or tough questioner. Don't start your Q&A on a negative note. Often the first question or two set the tone for the entire news conference. Now, I know I wrote in an earlier chapter, "Don't assume that you have friends in the media." Calling on someone who has been sympathetic in the past does not guarantee a gentle question, but the odds are better for you. A reporter who was sympathetic in the past *may* change her spots in a news conference, but you can almost bet that someone who has been antagonistic in the past will be antagonistic at your news conference as well.

¶ **Work the room.** When you are delivering your opening and closing statements and when you're answering questions, speak to the whole room. For questions, start your response looking at the reporter who asked you the question, express a thought, then move on to the reporters on your left, express a thought, turn your attention to the reporters on your right, and so on. Don't do a radar sweep of the room; you're not looking for incoming aircraft and you won't engage anyone that way.

Also, don't talk to a fixed spot in the room. As a reporter, I've been to a number of news conferences where the spokesperson addressed all his statements to a static spot at the back of the room. I once asked a back-of-the-room concentrator why he was doing that and he told me, "Well, I was told to always address my remarks to an imaginary clock on the back wall." Why talk to an imaginary clock when you have warm human bodies to address? Engage the people in the room.

If the question was a friendly one, work your way back and conclude your answer looking directly at the questioner. That way, if he's got a follow-up, you're in position to recognize him. If the question was a tough one, don't go back to him at the end of your answer. That way you can move on to someone else for the next question even if the tough questioner has a follow-up.

¶ **Keep an eye on the time.** If you told the assembled media that you'll take questions for fifteen minutes, and if the conference has been tough, after thirteen minutes have elapsed announce that time's almost up and you can take "one or two" additional questions. If things are going swimmingly, you can let the clock run a little longer before announcing you have time for one or two last queries. Use the *one or two* question phrase because it enables you to stop after one question. And that's what you should do if the first question is an easy one that accommodates one of your message points. If, however, the first question is a stinker, take a second one in an effort to go out on a positive note. If the second one is a stinker, too, answer it and end the session; things are unlikely to get any better.

¶ **End with a summary statement.** Thank the reporters for attending and deliver a summary of your most important points. Your closer should be a brief condensation of your opening remarks. Deliver it from memory, don't read it from a script.

The news conference is an invaluable tool in crisis communications. Many organizations prepare action plans for crises — readying an institutional response to various worst-case scenarios. No crisis plan is complete without a communication component. Whether the crisis you may face is an industrial accident with severe community-wide ramifications, an incident of workplace or school violence, a disease outbreak, an act of nature, or an act of terrorism, an essential part of your crisis response plan must be media communications. The next chapter deals with crisis communications, and I preface it with the hope that you never have to call on these tips and tools.

CRISIS COMMUNICATIONS: ARE YOU PREPARED FOR THE WORST-CASE SCENARIO?

On September 10, 2001, Rudolph Giuliani was the unpopular, weakened lame duck mayor of New York City. He was widely despised for his brusque, authoritarian manner which had grown more pronounced during his second term. His personal life was such a train wreck it had become fodder for latenight comedians. One day later, September 11, 2001, Rudolph Giuliani became the *de facto* spokesman of the United States; he was the face of authority and reassurance in the immediate aftermath of the terrorist attacks against the World Trade Center and the Pentagon.

The mayor went from being the butt of jokes to being a hero overnight thanks in large part to his skill in communicating about the unprecedented crisis. He rose to the occasion, convincingly conveying the breadth, scope, and severity of the attacks that took the lives of three thousand innocent people that awful day. He appeared to be a steady anchor and a compassionate captain in a confusing tempest. Giuliani had an advantage over President Bush, the officeholder one would have expected to be that anchor. Part of this advantage was due to Giuliani's proximity to the disaster — the World Trade Center was walking distance from New York's City Hall. The president, on the other hand, wasn't in Washington that day; prior scheduling had him at a photo-op in a second grade classroom in Sarasota, Florida, where he was promoting his education plan. Uncertainty about other attacks led the president on a zigzag course around the country and it wasn't until early evening that he returned to the White House. So for nearly twelve hours between the time the first plane hit the first tower and the time the president addressed the nation on live TV from the Oval Office, the New York mayor had the crisis communications stage largely to himself.

It is hard to believe that there was no national crisis plan for something like 9/11, but if there was, the media communications portion was missing or ignored. In New York, on the other hand, Mayor Giuliani may have been working from instinct, rather than from a plan, but his actions are instructive to us when we create a crisis communication strategy.

Four qualities in Giuliani's response stand out and they are essential for establishing and maintaining communications control in a crisis. They should be the basis of every crisis communications plan.

**GIULIANI'S 9/11
COMMUNICATIONS STRENGTHS**

**Early Response
Frequent and Uncomplicated Media Accessibility
Consistent Candor
Empathy**

It may be difficult to *plan* empathy, which is the emotional component of a spokesperson's response, but it is not hard to envision how the public might respond to a crisis. For our purposes, empathy in crises like a terrorist attack, a major natural disaster, an Isla Vista or Sandy Hook type shooting, or any other dire, life-threatening event, can be defined as seeing the event the same way the public does and addressing the public's predictable concerns. In crises, media outlets, which normally see themselves as writing the first draft of history, often add to their mandate the job of sharing national concern and bringing the public together. To fulfill that latter role the media are eager for high-ranking, empathetic crisis spokespersons. In the case of 9/11, it was Mayor Giuliani, who did everything right.

President Bush had another opportunity to take communications control of a crisis in 2005 when Hurricane Katrina struck the Gulf Coast and destroyed huge sections of New Orleans. But he blew the opportunity with a slow response and often less-than-empathetic statements. Bush had been on a five-week vacation at his ranch in Texas when the storm roared into the Gulf Coast. It took three full days before he flew over the affected areas for the first time and two more days before he set foot in the region. Worse, yet, during those days, the president left his ranch for previously planned photo-op side trips to Arizona and California to promote his plan for the Medicare drug benefit. His staff, concerned that Bush appeared indifferent to the suffering of tens of thousands in New Orleans, put together a DVD with all the news coverage and urged him to watch it so he would gain insight into the depth and breadth of the problem. But the president didn't watch the DVD until he was flying to New Orleans for his on-the-ground visit on September 2, five days after the storm struck. In addition to the delayed response, once Bush was on-scene in the devastated area, there were a number of serious communications gaffes. It was reported that Coast Guard rescue helicopters were diverted from their mission to serve as a backdrop for presidential photos. Another report said the presidential visit shut down the New Orleans airport, delaying delivery of three tons of needed food. Then, in fairly rapid succession over the course of just a few days, the president made these three statements:

**PRESIDENT GEORGE W. BUSH
IN KATRINA'S AFTERMATH**

"I am satisfied with the response. I am not satisfied with all the results."

"Heck of a job, Brownie," (directed to Michael Brown, the FEMA director whose agency was responding so poorly that nations around the world, including even U.S. archenemy *Cuba,* offered assistance)

And, on learning that Sen. Trent Lott's house had been destroyed: **"Out of the rubble of Trent Lott's house... there's going to be a fantastic house. And I'm looking forward to sitting on the porch."**

Time magazine characterized that last remark as "astonishingly tone-deaf to the homeless black citizens still trapped in the post apocalyptic water world of New Orleans."

Additionally, a day before his in-person visit, the president said, "I don't think anybody anticipated the breach of the levees." Video later made available to the media showed a tele-conference Mr. Bush attended the day before the storm hit in which a hurricane expert and FEMA Director Brown specifically warned that the levees might not hold if Katrina scored a direct hit on New Orleans. This supplies us with another teachable moment: don't deny what has been recorded — the video will always surface and embarrass you.

In the Katrina tragedy, the president ignored the Giuliani lessons of 9/11 — early response, frequent and uncomplicated media accessibility, consistent candor, and empathy. Building on Giuliani's success and Bush's gaffes, President Obama and New Jersey Gov. Chris Christie were quickly on the scene and expressing empathy with victims of Hurricane Sandy in 2012. It is critically important that in establishing your crisis communications plan you and your colleagues pay heed to those lessons, as Obama and Christie clearly did.

YOUR CRISIS MANAGEMENT PLAN COMES FIRST

Before you craft a crisis *communications* plan, you have to have a crisis *management* plan. If you don't have such a plan and you are ad-libbing your crisis response, then all the speed, accessibility and empathy in the world aren't going to help you. You will quickly be viewed as stage-managing the event — performing a smoke-and-mirrors act to mask your inadequate response. This is a lose-lose situation. In crises, there is no "which comes first, the chicken or the egg" question; the management plan comes first, the communications plan is hatched later. If you don't have a management plan, there is nothing to communicate.

Preparing a crisis management plan is outside the purview of this book and beyond my area of expertise, but I do know that the time to plan for a crisis is in advance and that every conceivable department or division that will respond in the crisis must be involved in the planning. A key to your crisis management plan's success will be communication, because most crises require some public response and unless there are adequate communications, the public won't know what to do. A crisis management plan without a communications component is just as futile as a crisis communications scheme without a crisis management plan.

INFORMATION THE PUBLIC NEEDS IN A CRISIS

Obviously, crises vary in degree, intensity, and effect on the public. A company's bankruptcy is a tragedy, one that deeply affects employees, customers, and stockholders. It might even have a ripple economic impact on a community or a region. Such a crisis, while devastating to those involved, is limited insofar as the affected population. The deadly swarm of tornadoes that killed more than a dozen people and did billions of dollars of damage to Arkansas and Mississippi in April 2014 were largely regional in their direct impact. The entire country felt deep sympathy for victims, but the threat and effects were not national. The 9/11 terrorist attacks and the subsequent anthrax mailings had far wider ripples. In the first, the American mainland suffered 3,000 killed in its first significant foreign attack since the War of 1812, and the threat of further terrorist strikes frightened millions. After anthrax-tainted letters began showing up, the previously benign mail slot in every American home suddenly became a potential portal for bio-terrorists.

Whatever the crisis, the pubic wants answers to four basic questions which your communications plan must address:

**WHAT THE PUBLIC WANTS TO KNOW
IN A CRISIS SITUATION**

Is this crisis dangerous physically or economically to me and my family?

If there is danger, what actions should we take to mitigate risks?

If there is no danger, how can we be of service to those in jeopardy?

What steps are you, the responders, taking to mitigate the crisis and to prevent a recurrence?

ADDITIONAL CRISIS INFORMATION

Answering the public's questions is a start, but the communications plan should also address key crisis management issues:

¶ **How will the response** contain the effects of the crisis.

¶ **How will responders** allocate mitigation and recovery resources equitably and fairly.

¶ **How crisis managers** plan to avoid wasting resources, including personnel, material, and funds.

WHO SPEAKS IN THE CRISIS; HOW THEY SHOULD SPEAK

¶ **Designate spokespersons in advance.** When a crisis breaks, you frequently see multiple spokespersons jostling for the media spotlight, trying to manage the communications. This is counterproductive because it sends a message that nobody is in charge. You may remember Secretary of State Alexander Haig's media response after would-be assassin John Hinckley, jr. wounded President Reagan. Haig announced to the White House reporters, "As of now, I'm in control here in the White House." In fact, he was not; the vice president, George H. W. Bush, was in charge, even though at that moment he was out of town. The Constitution provides a chain of succession and the Vice President, Speaker of the House of Representatives and President *Pro Tem* of the Senate are all in that chain. The Secretary of State is not. It remained for White House spokespersons and others who were more familiar with the laws of presidential succession than Haig, to straighten out the communications mess.

A good crisis communications plan designates spokespersons in advance. The fewer they are in number and the higher ranking they are in office, the better the plan. The more expert the spokespersons, the better. Both as a journalist and a member of the public, I don't want anyone telling me about an impending pandemic unless he has an M.D. after his name and is a very high official of a relevant agency or organization, such as the Centers for Disease Control. Hearing this information from a political appointee just doesn't reassure the public. And I certainly don't want to hear from a high-ranking physician who says, "A," and then hear from the political appointee saying, "B." All spokespersons need to be on the same page. If your agency or organization will need outside experts to vet your messages, recruit them in advance, brief them on your crisis management and communication plans, and enlist their cooperation and aid. If you fail to have experts at your disposal, the media will find other, often less-qualified, figures to interview.

In the absence of official communicators, the media will call everybody and anybody in an organization when a crisis breaks. It's imperative that the organization knows who the proper spokespersons are and refers reporters to them. If they don't, you'll face a flood tide of speculative statements to the media from people within your own organization who have only a partial picture of the crisis.

¶ **Get out in front of the crisis.** Late messages are as bad as mixed messages. Remember President Bush's response to hurricane Katrina? Not only was the impact of his message severely weakened, but also his late response damaged the perception of his leadership in that crisis. If you or your spokesperson doesn't get out and address the crisis quickly, other "experts," many of them self-appointed and ill-informed, will assume the mantle of authority. After the 9/11 attacks, Americans wondered if they should buy gas masks as a precaution against possible chemical attacks by terrorists. It took the federal government three weeks to come up with the recommendation to not buy them. During these weeks, self-appointed terrorism experts filled the interview chairs on the 24-hour news channels, warning of the dangers of chemical weapons. In the aftermath of this onslaught of fear-based ruminating, the public depleted Army/Navy stores and online military surplus companies of every gas mask on their shelves.

If you don't respond in a timely manner, someone else will, and it may prove hard to wrest back control of crisis communications once that horse is out of the barn. Remember this: into any information vacuum, the media will suck up and then disseminate rumor and speculation from publicity-hungry "experts" who readily, even eagerly, make themselves available.

¶ **Empathy, not paternalism.** Another cardinal sin of crisis communications harkens back to our Commandment 5: "Thou shalt not lie, evade, speculate, nor *cop an attitude*." Copping a paternalistic attitude is the flip side of empathy in crisis communication. If you can't communicate without talking down to people, don't talk to them at all. If you are paternalistic, everything you say will be disbelieved or resented. The most common form of paternalism is withholding bad news from the public for fear it will panic or react badly. Eventually the information is going to come out and once it does, your credibility will be in shambles. The public can handle bad news if you present it in a mature, factual, respectful way. A series of 55 focus groups conducted across the country by the Centers for Disease Control and five universities found that uncertainty is more difficult to deal with than bad news and that *any* information is empowering in a crisis.

¶ **Don't speculate.** Again, we're revisiting Commandment 5. Speculation develops a life of its own; a very long life, in fact. Even if your speculation is partially right, it's dangerous because the the wrong part poisons the correct information.

¶ **Put out the fires of rumor.** Wild rumors accompany nearly every crisis, especially in our Twitter, texting, Facebook age. If you do not quickly bat down rumors with facts, they grow like viruses and once a rumor virus gains hold, it infects all discourse about the crisis. So it's imperative to move quickly to squelch rumors. Many Americans believed rumors of mass rapes of women and girls in the Superdome in the aftermath of Katrina. It didn't happen, but authorities did not refute the rumors in a timely manner and as a result, years later many still believe and repeat the rape stories.

¶ **Show your credentials.** A small group of protesters stirred up fear in the Florida communities near the Kennedy Space Center during the run-up to the launch of a spacecraft because it carried some 70 pounds of plutonium to power its instruments. The government spokespersons working to reassure the public about these fears gained greater credibility from their academic credentials than from their bureaucratic titles. I urged one government spokespersons to work into all her interviews the fact that she was an MIT-educated engineer who had written her master's thesis on nuclear safety. That was a lot more reassuring to the media and to the public than her official government title.

¶ **Don't answer what you can't answer. Do answer what you can answer.** "I don't know. We're working on it," is a perfectly valid answer, especially if followed by a description of what steps are being taken to work on the question. On the other hand, don't withhold information, unless it is critically important to do so. Trying to manage a crisis by hiding facts is usually fruitless at best and counterproductive at worst. As Shakespeare wrote in *The Merchant of Venice*, "Truth will out." When it does, your credibility plummets and you find yourself managing both a crisis and a credibility gap. But what about information you really can't share? Respectfully tell the public that you are withholding some information and why you are withholding it. If you have no results to report, talk about the process that will lead to results. The public wants to know *something* is being done, even if it hasn't yet borne fruit.

KEEP YOUR SPOKESPERSONS IN THE LOOP

Part of your crisis communications plan must include mechanisms for keeping spokespersons informed. They cannot address public concerns if they don't know what's going on. Never withhold information from your spokespersons because you want it withheld from the public. If that information gets out and the spokesperson did not know about it, he no longer has any credibility with the media. "I can't discuss that; it's an ongoing process, and until we get results we don't want to speculate," is a better answer than, "I *didn't* know that."

A crisis communications plan must designate a team to decide what information to release and what to withhold. You can't begin scrambling to put together that team once a crisis breaks; everyone will be too busy. Designated crisis team members should understand in advance that their management duties include serving on the communications team, and that they'll need to be available. Also well in advance, the team must learn the demands and needs of both the public and the media, so that they don't revert to the all too familiar response of clamming up in the face of adversity. The instinct of any organization is to protect itself and often that involves withholding information. Crisis management teams may find it easier to withhold information than to do the hard work of considering what to release and when to release it. This policy is self-defeating and it's important the crisis communications team, from top to bottom, understand that.

At this point you may feel as if you're ready to confront any media opportunity with confidence. But not so fast! Let's take the last chapter to review the basics and determine if you are ready for *your* fifteen minutes of fame.

GETTING READY FOR
YOUR FIFTEEN MINUTES

During the first year of "Good Morning America," the show's talent coordinators booked an interview with James Cagney. Cagney, one of Hollywood's original tough guy gangster stars, was then in poor health and lived a reclusive life with his wife on a farm about two hours north of New York City. He had not made a movie nor given an interview in 15 years, so booking him was a real coup. A group of us — David Hartman, two camera crews, director Jan Rifkinson and one or two others — drove to his farm one afternoon and David sat down with the screen legend for about two hours of conversation.

At one point, Hartman asked Cagney the secret of his extraordinarily natural acting style. In his staccato New York Irish accent, Cagney said, "Nothin' to it. Ya walk in, look the other fella in the eye, an' say yer lines." With those few words Cagney distilled not only acting but also media interviews. If you, as a spokesperson, are prepared, there should be "nothin' to it." You ought to be able to "look the other fella in the eye an' say yer lines." In this case the "other fella" is a reporter and your agenda is "yer lines."

If you got to this page by reading the previous eleven chapters — and not by flipping to the end to see how it all turns out — then you have a good sense of what you need to do prepare to look that "other fella in the eye."

Let's review the basics of interview preparation:

THE FIVE COMMANDMENTS

Commandment 1. Thou shalt be prepared. Knowing what you want to say in advance of an interview is the key to media mastery. If you do not establish an agenda for each interview, you will be at the mercy of the reporter's agenda. Even when the reporter's agenda matches your own, you are cheating yourself out of an opportunity to be most effective if you don't prepare a set of messages in advance of the interview. And remember our Law of Interviews: *Anybody unprepared for tough questions will be asked them.* If you prepare for the worst it's unlikely a reporter will blindside you in the interview. Also, as close to interview time as possible, check Google for the latest news about you, your company, your project, and your industry. You don't want the reporter surprising you with the bombshell of a new development during your interview.

Commandment 2: Thou shalt know thy Listener. You are not talking *to* the reporter. You are talking *through* her to her readers, viewers, or listeners. No matter how conversational a reporter is with you, she is working. You should be working, too. Your job is to reach her audience with your agenda points.

Commandment 3: Thou shalt be quoteworthy. To reach that audience you have to communicate in ways that are so compelling the reporter says to herself, "I gotta use that." Express your agenda points comprehensively, with economy, and in memorable language. Most good interview subjects are thought-provoking and speak with a deft ease that appears innate but more often than not is a result of extensive preparation. Use grabbers (word pictures, analogies, comparisons, and other colorful word devices) to turn agenda points into soundbites. The ideal soundbite is no more than thirty words long, takes no more than ten seconds to speak, and is no more than three sentences long. Incorporate the sense of an interviewer's question in your answer so your quote or soundbite can stand on its own and doesn't need an introduction from the reporter.

Commandment 4: Thou shalt practice, practice, practice. It is a not enough to prepare, you must also practice. Read your agenda points out loud to see if they work. Sometimes you won't be able to get your mouth around the phrases you've written; you don't want to learn that in the middle of a broadcast interview with a microphone recording your every word. The more you practice, the more comfortable you will be with your messages, and the more natural and conversational you'll make them in an interview. Have someone throw questions at you; it's better to hear them coming from another voice than to ask them of yourself. Record, review, and critique your practice sessions.

Commandment 5: Thou shalt not lie, evade, speculate, nor cop an attitude. Abraham Lincoln was right when he said, "It is true that you may fool all the people some of the time; you can even fool some of the people all of the time; but you cannot fool all of the people all of the time." Untruths and half-truths usually pop up like an insufficiently weighted victim a mob hit man dropped in a lake. Insofar as attitude, if you alienate your audience it will reject your agenda.

BEFORE, DURING, AND AFTER THE INTERVIEW

To obey these five commandments, you will need to take some concrete steps before, during, and after any interview. Failing to take all these steps doesn't guarantee doom, but taking them goes a long way toward ensuring success. If you think of an interview as a performance, these steps equate to creating your material, rehearsing it, performing it, and then following up to insure you and the audience members are happy with the performance.

Before the Interview

¶ **Determine your agenda.** Create an agenda for the interview and craft your Positive Message Statements. When you write them out, keep in mind that your audience is not the reporter, but her readers, viewers, or listeners. Make your points come alive with grabbers; they enhance your agenda and entice reporters and the public. Remember, when you are writing your messages and your grabbers, your end-users are always asking themselves, "Why should I care?" Answer that question somewhere in your agenda.

¶ **List your nightmare questions.** Figure out the worst questions any reporter can ask you and tie one of your agenda points to each of those questions. Study these question-and-answer links: they will be your mental road map from a tough question to an answer that serves your agenda.

¶ **Check out the media outlet.** Make an effort to learn the reporter's likely agenda. Research what her publication or broadcast is like. Does it have a particular style or point of view? How might that point of view influence her reporting on your organization? How detailed does the outlet get? Does it address a sophisticated or a general audience? What is the individual reporter's style in an interview? There are five questions to ask the reporter who will be interviewing you:

1. What is the direction or thrust of the story?
2. Who else are you interviewing?

3. How much of my time will you need?
4. How long will your article (or broadcast story) run?
5. Do you need or want any documentation, photos graphics, or videotape?

¶ **Rehearse.** Before any interview, you'll want to practice, practice, practice. Rehearse your responses to challenging questions. Have a colleague or friend aggressively throw questions at you so you get used to answering with your agenda points. Record these practice sessions and study your performance. Give yourself a point for every agenda message you worked in. Take away a point for every one you failed to include. Repeat the exercise until you have a perfect score.

¶ **Be informed.** As close to the time of the interview as possible, check Google for the latest news. Check opponents' web sites to see what they are saying.

¶ **Arrive early and warm up.** Arrive at the venue early and establish yourself with the reporter during a preinterview warmup so she thinks of you as a human being. Use the warm-up to plant the seeds of your agenda points with her, even deploying grabbers in the warm-up; perhaps they'll grow into questions.

DURING THE INTERVIEW
¶ **Answer in complete sentences.** Think of an answer as an island — standing independent of anything you've said earlier in the interview and even independent of the reporter's question. To do that you'll want to include the sense of the question in your answer. (The one exception to the rule: a hostile question containing negative language; the "disaster waiting to happen" question.)

¶ **Record the interview.** You want a record of what you said and how you said it. If it's a television interview, record it on video. For other media encounters, audio recording is sufficient. Also, bring a witness; someone from your organization who knows the subject area of the interview. He'll be available to correct you if you inadvertently misspeak during the Q&A.

¶ **Use Counterintuitive Communications.** An interview is not a conversation, so I have four fundamental rules that are conversationally counterintuitive:

1. KPUF — Key Point Up Front. Lead with your strongest stuff. This is the way the media speaks to us and it is the way we should speak to the media

2. KISS — Keep it Short and Simple. Remember our 30/10/3 rule — soundbites should be no more than thirty words, take no more than ten seconds to speak, and should be no more than three sentences. As to how simple, if you're dealing with a general audience, use the national average grade level: tenth grade. But for highly emotional and controversial subjects, communicate at the sixth grade level.

3. KOTJ — Knock off The Jargon. Activate your jargon filter. Avoid acronyms and other verbal short-cuts. You and your colleagues will understand what you're saying but the rest of us will be left scratching our heads as we attempt to translate your remarks into English.

4. Brand. If it's got a name, use it. It's not "we" or "us," it's the name of your organization. If you're talking about a book, a product, or a policy, use its title or name.

¶ **Stay cool.** Remain calm during the interview; your attitude counts even in print interviews where the reader won't see your face. When writing her story, a print reporter can characterize you as appearing nervous or furtive. If you are prepared with your own agenda, it's easier to be calm and resolute.

¶ **Everything is on the record.** Don't go off the record, supply any information on a not-for-attribution basis, or ever use the phrase, "No comment." If you can't answer a question, explain why you can't and then offer to help the reporter find someone who can answer it. Then tell her what you *can* talk about.

¶ **Stick to your agenda.** Most people are taught to be polite, so it is easy to get sidetracked onto the reporter's agenda by dutifully answering her questions. This is fine if her agenda meshes with yours, but that won't always be the case, so keep your agenda at the forefront of your thoughts and work your answers around to it. Use our four steps to get back on track from her off-the-point or tough questions:

    1. Short form answer. You must acknowledge her question or she will ask it again.

    2. Build a bridge. Just a few words can get you beyond your short form answer and leave you on the threshold of your agenda. Use simple words or phrases for your bridges like: "on the other hand," "in fact," "however," "but," or "and."

    3. State your agenda point. Cross that bridge and move on to one of your points. State it at greater length than your short form answer and anchor it with a grabber.

    4. Shut up. You don't want to add the anti-climactic, "And that's why...." and restate her off-point or hostile question.

¶ **Flag it.** The longer it takes you to get to that bridge, the less likely you are to cross it to your agenda. If you find yourself going on at great length in step one, here's a way to recover: flag your agenda point. Simply say, "The most important thing to remember is...." or "what I really want to say is...." and move on to your PMS. This alerts both reporter and the public that you're really getting to the meat of your answer. Flagging also works well if you find yourself violating the KISS rule — keep it short and simple. If you're going on and on and on, just focus attention on what you *really* want to say by flagging. Flagging is inelegant, but it works.

¶ **Be specific.** The media — and their audiences — love specifics. It is easy to infer the general from the specific, while it is impossible to infer the specific from the general. "A lot of money" means a very different amount to Warren Buffett than it does to me. But if you say $10 million, both he and I know exactly what you're talking about and we can categorize it as "a lot of money," in my case and "a rounding error," in his.

¶ **Enumerate.** If there are three pieces of evidence that support your contention, announce that there are three of them and then tick them off one-by-one. Audiences respond to enumeration. It is more effective to say "there are three benefits," and then list them, than to speak about the same three benefits randomly.

¶ **Know when your interview ends.** An interview is over after the reporter or you leave the premises, not after the notebook, recorder, or camera is put away. As long as you are in the presence of a reporter, she is observing and mentally recording. The whole world may read or hear anything you say in proximity to a reporter or a microphone. In fact, anything you say in proximity to a reporter — even in a nonworking venue — may be grist for her mill. In 2001, at a party hosted by Conrad Black, one of Britain's major newspaper publishers and filled with journalists, France's ambassador to the United Kingdom undiplomatically told the guests he thought Israel was, "A *&$@# little country." Naturally, the story broke in the British papers, which exhibited far less reticence about using his actual word than I did. Instead of apologizing, the diplomat said, "I thought this was a social occasion." The ambassador's belief that he could say something so provocative in front of newspeople without being quoted was stunningly naïve. There are no private moments with journalists.

¶ **If you don't understand a question, don't answer it.** Ask the reporter to rephrase it. Or you can rephrase it yourself, "Bill, if I understand your question, you want to know…."

¶ **Watch your words and the reporter's words.** Don't repeat loaded or negative words in a question. "Isn't this a disaster waiting to happen?" is designed to elicit from you:"This isn't a disaster waiting to happen." Don't say it!

AFTER THE INTERVIEW
¶ **Be cooperative.** Offer the reporter the opportunity to fact check her article or her broadcast script with you; you are not asking for approval rights over her story, just offering to confirm the facts.

¶ **Review your recording.** Screen or listen to your recording of the interview immediately after the reporter leaves. If you discover you misspoke, call her up and tell her you made a mistake and correct it. If you've omitted a key message point, call her up and tell her that her readers or listeners might want to know about one more point. Reporters won't hesitate to phone you if they come up with more questions while writing their story; you should feel free to call them and volunteer information you may not have gotten into the interview.

If you're dissatisfied with your performance, analyze what you did wrong. Every time you watch or listen to that recording, you're learning how to do it right the next time.

¶ **Complain if you've been treated unfairly.** If you feel a reporter has misrepresented you, complain. Reporters with a pattern of misrepresentation need to be held accountable. On the other hand, if the story was tough but fair, don't waste your time complaining, it could backfire.

MANAGING NERVES

If you are nervous, you may get sloppy, forget your agenda and fall back on verbal tics, like "y'know" and "actually."

One way to conquer nerves is to be prepared. But even the best-prepared sometimes feel unduly apprehensive in an interview. Here's a breathing exercise that should slow down your heart rate and help you concentrate on the job at hand:

Breathe in through your nose for three seconds. Fill your lungs. Hold the breath for three seconds. Breathe out through your mouth for three seconds. Empty your lungs. Repeat this three times.

That 27-second exercise should calm you.

If you pepper your answers with "y'know," "y'know what I mean," "actually" and "like," you will sound unsure of yourself and undermine your authority. These are verbal tics that are manifestations of nervousness or sloppy verbal habits found even among well-educated and articulate people. Sometimes we are so reliant on them and deploy them so much they become distracting. I had a media training client who once used "actually" four times in a single sentence: "Actually we actually will actually fly this plane and it actually will help us with our program." I told her that in Hollywood, "actually" means "I'm lying to you" as in, "He's actually out of the office" which everyone in show business knows means he's in the office and won't talk to you. That helped a little, but there is a remedy that you should try cautiously because it either cures the problem or makes it far worse. Attempt it before a practice interview, to see what your response is, don't try it for the first time when you are going to sit down with Brian Williams of NBC News. The technique: Repeat the offending word as many times as you can in thirty seconds. Do it with a timer going. If your tic is "y'know," repeat "Y'know, y'know, y'know, y'know" at a brisk pace for half a minute. As I said this will either cure you or kill you, and that's why it's important to do it in a practice session. If it doesn't help, another trick is to record yourself in an interview and stop the playback every time you deploy your verbal tic. This will dramatize to you just how distracting and harmful it is.

DO YOU NEED
PROFESSIONAL MEDIA TRAINING?

There are a lot of companies and individuals offering media training, and you may want to avail yourself of the services of one of them. One way to tell if you need training is to write up a series of Positive Message Statements and a series of challenging questions and then have a friend or colleague interview you. (You'll want him to read "Reporters' top Eight Dirty Tricks" in Chapter 4 before grilling you.) Record the session on video and study it to see how successful you were at working your PMSs into the interview. The cosmetics of your response are less important than your ability to work agenda points into your answers. Give yourself a point for every PMS you work into the interview. Deduct one for every PMS on your list that you failed to deploy. Did you score zero or less? You probably need training. If you got all your points in, you may be a natural and not need training unless you are expecting exceptionally tough interviews. If you scored somewhere in the middle, assess your performance, and decide if a professional trainer can improve it. Finally, if you are booked to do an investigative TV newsmagazine show, you need media training no matter how good you are in other interview settings.

Normally, only you can answer the question of whether or not you need training. If the answer is "yes," you may find it tempting to have an in-house public relations person train you. My experience has been that most of them really don't want to do it. And with good reason. More often than not, a staffer should not do this sort of training. First, they may not be qualified. Second, if they work for you they may be extremely shy about giving you the proper grilling with tough, squirm-in-your-seat questions. And they may go easy on you when critiquing your performance. In-house personnel may also know too much, so when you respond in your organization's shorthand code, they will understand and let you get away with it, whereas an outside trainer will point out that you are failing to communicate beyond your own community.

The best advice is to look outside your organization and find a qualified and trustworthy group or individual. The qualified credential is self-evident, but the trustworthy is equally important because you may be revealing to this outsider intimate and potentially damaging information about you, your business, or your organization. Even if you don't intend to disclose proprietary information during training, I find clients often reveal such details inadvertently. So engage the services of a media trainer whose first loyalty is to you as a client, not to the calling of journalism. I have been summoned to media train around the country because clients feared their local trainers might share with media friends sensational information disclosed during a workshop. I feel that if a trainer is untrustworthy some of the time, he is untrustworthy all of the time. å

QUESTIONS TO ASK
A PROSPECTIVE MEDIA TRAINER

1. What are you training me for?
2. What materials do you leave behind?
3. Do you have a confidentiality agreement?
4. What is your background?

¶ **What are you training me for?** If the first word out of the trainer's mouth is "television," I would find someone else, unless you are going to appear *only* on television. Most people need training for *media* interviews, encounters, and presentations, not just for television. A media trainer who answers "television" is likely to stress the unique cosmetic considerations of the one-eyed beast over the *substance* you need to develop for all media interviews. Any coach you engage should customize the curriculum to meet your needs. For example, if it is highly unlikely you'll ever suffer an ambush by a TV crew, why waste a valuable chunk of training time with an ambush exercise?

¶ **What sort of materials do you leave behind?** Believe it or not, some media trainers collect the video of your interviews and other training materials when the session ends, claiming those are proprietary to the trainer. This means you can't review your performance further to learn from your mistakes. Reviewing interviews and training materials is important when you are preparing for interviews. Moreover, those worksheets likely contain your most feared questions and the videos your most embarrassing slips of the tongue made in practice interviews. You want that material securely in your own hands, not in the hands of an outsider, even if the outsider has signed a confidentiality agreement. Which brings us to our next question:

¶ **Do you have a confidentiality agreement to insure my organization's secrets will be protected?** This question should be unnecessary. Any trustworthy trainer will offer you a confidentiality agreement in his initial conversation with you; you should not have to ask about one. Confidentiality should be as high a priority for him as it is for you. Even if your organization has its own confidentiality agreement, I would ask that question in the event the trainer does not offer the information voluntarily. Avoid any media coach who lacks his own confidentiality agreement or one who declines to sign your agreement. A trainer without his own confidentiality agreement may be insensitive to the need to protect his clients. If you do require your media coach to sign a confidentiality agreement, be certain any colleagues who join him sign as well.

¶ **What is your background?** There is no hard-and-fast rule that someone must have media experience to be a media trainer, but it certainly helps a trainer get inside the head of a reporter if he has been a reporter. Some media trainers today are former actors, public relations representatives, and marketing personnel with no direct, hands-on media experience. Some others are media "veterans" whose experience was at the lowest, nonreporting, noninterviewing, nonwriting levels. Some of these may be good, despite the lack of direct media experience. But how confident would you be if the pilot of your transatlantic airliner came on the intercom and said, "This is Captain Jones and my background is in aviation. I used to work the check-in counter and then I was a baggage-handler before becoming a pilot. Oh, and this is my first flight, so sit back, relax, and enjoy the ride."

Ask yourself, "Do I really want someone with no reporting experience playing reporter in my media training? Do I want someone who specializes in marketing to prepare me for '60 Minutes' type questions?" The ideal trainer need not have multimedia experience. Although a print interviewer's techniques are quite different, and in some cases are far more seductive than a broadcast reporter's techniques, journalists understand that and many can play either role. With the ranks of newspapers dwindling, it is becoming increasingly difficult to find media trainers with both print and broadcast experience. If you are going to be doing interviews with various media, you want training from an expert whose background is extensive and who understands multiple media, even if he hasn't worked in all of them.

INDIVIDUAL OR GROUP TRAINING

Normally, I prefer groups. For the client they are highly cost-effective. And even if money is no object, participants in group sessions learn a lot by watching each other — picking up pointers from colleagues' hits and misses. Also, a group is likely to come up with more good Positive Message Statements, more grabbers, and more tough questions than an individual. One-on-one training can take considerably less time, however — principally because the solo player is the only one interviewed and critiqued. Solo training is appropriate when the workshop deals with a unique crisis that only one spokesperson will address or when prepping a spokesperson for a hostile or challenging investigative broadcast interview.

It's best to conduct the training away from your personal office, far from the temptation of email inboxes, phones, and importuning subordinates and colleagues. A conference room — preferably on a different floor than your office — can work well. A hotel meeting room a couple of miles away from your headquarters is even better because there's no way a colleague can stroll in to interrupt with some bit of "can't wait" information. A number of my clients have their own small insert TV studios for public relations videos. These are ideal if sealed off from the normal business of the day.

During the training — as during all media interviews — turn off phones and Blackberries. I had one client who couldn't turn off his cell phone during training because he was expecting to get word on a big deal at any moment. He spent the better part of the day taking and placing calls and, indeed, concluded the big deal. Unfortunately, he was ill-equipped to announce it to the media.

Media training does not end with the final PowerPoint slide of a workshop or with the closing of this book. Like any other educational experience, it prepares you for further independent study. Sometimes, before a big event or a specific interview, you'll want a refresher with your trainer. Otherwise, keep your agenda points fresh, come up with new and better grabbers for them, and to do on-camera practice interviews with colleagues before embarking on a real interview.

Media mastery takes time and work. Few of us are natural spokespersons. But if you're going to do media interviews, the effort will result in unique opportunities. The more you work at it, the better you'll be at it. Not devoting the time and doing the work means you'll be the media's puppet or even — in extreme cases — their victim. Your investment of time and effort will pay dividends and empower you to speak through the media to the audience you really want to reach.

ABOUT THE AUTHOR

For three decades, George Merlis has used his print and broadcast news experience as the basis for media training hundreds of clients. As a TV producer, Merlis has overseen more than 10,000 broadcast interviews, the vast majority of them live. As a print journalist and investigative television news producer, he has conducted hundreds more interviews himself.

Merlis was executive producer of two of the three network morning shows, "Good Morning America" and "The CBS Morning News." He was also executive producer of the nationally syndicated "Entertainment Tonight" and USA Network's early venture into talk TV, "The Dick Cavett Show." Merlis has worked closely with talents as diverse in style as Ted Koppel, Diane Sawyer, David Hartman, Sam Donaldson, Geraldo Rivera, Gary Collins, Harry Reasoner, Bill Kurtis, Frank Reynolds, Bill Moyers, Peter Jennings, Barbara Walters, and Willard Scott.

His media training firm, Experience Media Consulting (www.MasterTheMedia.com) has trained a wide gamut of spokespersons ranging from rock stars to rocket scientists and most categories in between.

Earlier in his media career, as a print reporter and editor at the *New York World-Telegram and The Sun*, the *New York World Journal Tribune,* and the New York *Daily News*, Merlis covered a variety of subjects and wrote hundreds of news stories. In August, 1961, he was in Berlin to cover the building of the infamous wall which divided the city. Twenty-eight years later, as a TV producer for ABC, he came full cycle on the story when he went back to Berlin to cover the destruction of the wall and the collapse of East Germany.

Merlis began working in television in 1967 when he joined ABC News. He served on the large network team that covered the Apollo 11 mission to the moon. He was also an investigative producer on ABC's "The Reasoner Report," where he wrote, directed, and produced major stories about the food, chemical, petroleum, pharmaceutical, and automotive industries. He was also "The Reasoner Report's" environmental specialist.

Merlis won a 1999 National Emmy Award as executive producer, writer and director of the syndicated television program "Better Homes & Gardens." He also executive produced five long-running series for the Home and Garden Television network. Merlis produced a number of shows for Discovery Communications' networks, including the flagship Discovery Channel, the Science Channel, and the Travel Channel. For PBS, Merlis directed the lively panel show "Closer to Truth."

He wrote a novel, *VP,* and the nonfiction books *How to Make the Most of Every Media Appearance* and *How to Master the Media.* He co-wrote *Al Ubell's Energy Saving Guide for Homeowners* and a second book on a similar theme: *Save Energy, Save Money.* He writes a monthly bog about media mastery: http://www.MasterTheMedia.com/blog.

MEDIA MASTERY
WORKSHEETS
WORKSHEET 1 - PMSs

List five Positive Message Statements you want to work into your next interview.

1._____

_____

2._____

_____

3._____

_____

4._____

_____

5._____

_____

WORKSHEET 2 - WSIC

Fine-tune your PMSs to answer the public's "Why Should I Care" question. Characterize why they should care about at least one of your PMSs and ideally about all five.

1._____

_____

2._____

_____

3._____

_____

4._____

_____

5._____

_____

WORKSHEET 3 - GRABBERS

Create a grabber for each of your five PMSs. A grabber is a
word picture or other verbal device that makes your message
point come alive, turns it into a soundbite or a pull quote.

1._____

_____

2._____

_____

3._____

_____

4._____

_____

5._____

_____

WORKSHEET 4 TOUGH QUESTIONS

List your nightmare questions — those you find extremely tough to answer. After each question, write the PMS and grabber you want to navigate to in your answer.

Question:_____

_____

PMS to use in answer: _____

_____

_____

Question:_____

_____

PMS to use in answer:_____

_____

_____

Question:_____

_____

PMS to use in answer:_____

_____

Question:_____

_____

PMS to use in answer:_____

_____

_____

_____

Question:_____

_____

PMS to use in answer:_____

_____

_____

BRIDGING
THE FOUR STEPS TO YOUR AGENDA

1. Short form answer.
2. Build a bridge ("but," "however," "on the other hand.")
3. Deploy an agenda point and grabber
4. Shut up! Don't refer back to the original question.

NOTES

INDEX